Within Us

touchstones
Within Us

edited by

HENRY J. BARON
BRUCE HEKMAN
DANIEL VANDER ARK

The National Union of Christian Schools

William B. Eerdmans Publishing Company
Grand Rapids, Michigan

ISBN 0-8028-1533-2.

HENRY J. BARON received his B.A. from Calvin College, his M.A. from the University of Michigan, and his Ph.D. from the University of Illinois.

Dr. Baron taught in grades 5-12 at Sumas Christian School, Sumas, Washington, and South Christian High School, Grand Rapids, Michigan. He has taught classes at Grand Rapids Junior College, Grand Valley State College, and the University of Illinois and is presently Assistant Professor of English at Calvin College.

Author and editor of several articles, monographs, and curriculum guides, Dr. Baron is director of the *TOUCHSTONES* project and Language Arts Consultant for the National Union of Christian Schools.

BRUCE HEKMAN received his B.A. from Calvin College, his M.A. from the University of Michigan, and his Ph.D. from the University of Illinois.

Dr. Hekman taught at South Christian High School in Grand Rapids, Michigan. He is presently teaching and chairing the English Department at Chicago Christian High School, Palos Heights, Illinois.

Author of several articles and NUCS curriculum publications, Dr. Hekman has also conducted workshops and research in English programs for NUCS secondary schools.

DANIEL VANDER ARK earned his B.A. from Calvin College and his M.A. from the University of Nebraska.

Mr. Vander Ark teaches at Holland Christian High School, where he is chairman of the English Department. He is an author of four of the NUCS nine-week units in high school language arts: *Man and the Outcast, Man in Search of Self, Man in Search of Spiritual Significance,* and *The Language of Man.*

Editorial services and design were provided by Sandra L. Vander Zicht, NUCS Curriculum Editor, and by Jon Pott, Marlin Van Elderen, Milton Essenburg, and Joel Beversluis of the Wm. B. Eerdmans Publishing Company.

The work presented herein was developed by the NUCS Curriculum Department, supported by a grant from the Christian School Educational Foundation.

CONTENTS

PREFACE

TOUCHSTONES began as a revision of *THE PILOT SERIES IN LITERATURE, Book Three,* published by the NUCS in 1964. *TOUCHSTONES'* editors wrote a teacher's guide for *Book Three* in 1970, entitled *Thematic Literature Units 9,* in which they suggested many new selections and a new organizational pattern. This pattern developed the four themes now used in the *TOUCHSTONES* series: "Around Us," "Within Us," "Between Us," and "Above Us." *TOUCHSTONES* incorporates additional new selections, a modified version of the thematic organization, and new photos in a convenient and flexible format.

Underlying this new text is the conviction that curriculum materials should exhibit as equally as possible three major dimensions of Christian education—intellectual, decisional, and creative. We trust that the literature in *TOUCHSTONES* will promote personal growth along these lines. Through the thematic and generic focus in each book, the student can grow intellectually by learning about universal human experiences and concerns and about the artist's craft. As he is caught up in the tensions and conflicts of literature, he can grow in the attitudes and values that so strongly influence basic decisions in life. And he can grow creatively by responding to the literature in his own speaking, writing, and acting.

HENRY J. TRIEZENBERG, Ph.D.
NUCS Curriculum Administrator

DONALD OPPEWAL, Ph.D.
NUCS Policy Consultant

PHOTO CREDITS

Steven Friedman, pp. 3, 15, 41, 82, 181, 192, 219
H. Armstrong Roberts, pp. 6, 27
Dave Pott, p. 33
Paul Stoub, p. 137
Bruce Hekman, pp. 200, 215

ILLUSTRATIONS

Original drawings by Armand Merizon, pp. 13, 47, 107, 165

ACKNOWLEDGMENTS

"Dreams" by Langston Hughes. From *The Dream Keeper*. Copyright © 1932 by Alfred A. Knopf, Inc. Reprinted by permission of Harold Ober Associates Incorporated.

"Dream Deferred." Copyright 1951 by Langston Hughes. From *The Panther and the Lash* by Langston Hughes. Reprinted by permission of Alfred A. Knopf, Inc.

"The Secret Life of Bernard Twitchett" by Margaret Howard (with apologies to James Thurber). © 1970 by Scholastic Magazines, Inc. Reprinted by permission of Scholastic Magazines, Inc.

"Life for My Child," Part II of "The Womanhood." Copyright 1949 by Gwendolyn Brooks Blakely. By permission of Harper & Row, Publishers, Inc.

"Ride a Wild Horse" (original title: "Into the Sun") by Hannah Kahn. From *Saturday Review* (March 21, 1953). Copyright 1953 The Saturday Review Associates, Inc.

"The Skeptic" by Ruby Luse. From *Scholastic Scope*. © 1966 by Scholastic Magazines, Inc. Reprinted by permission of Scholastic Magazines, Inc.

"Charles." Copyright 1948, 1949 by Shirley Jackson. From *The Lottery* by Shirley Jackson. Reprinted with the permission of Farrar, Straus & Giroux, Inc.

"The Fifty-Yard Dash." Copyright 1938, 1964 by William Saroyan. Abridged by permission of Harcourt Brace Jovanovich, Inc. from "The Fifty-Yard Dash" in *My Name Is Aram* by William Saroyan.

"Echo and Narcissus," "Phaëthon," and "Daedalus," from *Mythology* by Edith Hamilton. Copyright 1942 by Edith Hamilton. Copyright renewed © 1969 by Dorian Fielding Reid. Copyright renewed © 1969 by Doris Fielding Reid, Executrix of the will of Edith Hamilton. By permission of Little, Brown and Company.

"The Cement Truck" by Laurence Lasky. From *Scholastic Scope*. © 1966 by Scholastic Magazines, Inc. Reprinted by permission of Scholastic Magazines, Inc.

"Me" by Marian Krell. From *Scholastic Scope.* © 1969 by Scholastic Magazines, Inc. Reprinted by permission of Scholastic Magazines, Inc.

"We Real Cool." Copyright © 1956 by Gwendolyn Brooks Blakely. By permission of Harper & Row, Publishers, Inc.

"My Financial Career," from *Literary Lapses* by Stephen Leacock. Reprinted by permission of Dodd, Mead & Company and of the Canadian publishers, McClelland & Stewart, Toronto. Certain changes have been made in this selection, with the permission of the original publishers.

"Abe Lincoln Grows Up." Adapted from *Abe Lincoln Grows Up* by Carl Sandburg. Copyright, 1926, 1928 by Harcourt Brace Jovanovich, Inc.; copyright, 1954, 1956 by Carl Sandburg. Reprinted by permission of the publisher.

"Sympathy," from *The Complete Poems of Paul Laurence Dunbar* by Paul Laurence Dunbar. Reprinted by permission of Dodd, Mead & Company.

"The Rescue of the Perishing" by William Saroyan. From *The Whole Voyald and Other Stories.* Reprinted by permission of the author.

"The Summer of Truth" by Lucile Vaughan Payne. Copyright © 1955 by Lucile Vaughan Payne. Appeared originally in *Seventeen.* Reprinted by permission of McIntosh and Otis, Inc.

"Absolute-ly." Reprinted from *Listen to the Green* by Luci Shaw. © 1971 by Harold Shaw Publishers, Box 567, Wheaton, IL 60187. Used by permission.

"The Conversion of Paul" (Acts 9), from *The Living Bible.* Reprinted by permission of Tyndale House Publishers.

"All the Years of Her Life" by Morley Callaghan. Copyright 1935, 1962 Morley Callaghan. Originally appeared in *The New Yorker.* Reprinted by permission of the Harold Matson Company, Inc.

"When I Was One-and-Twenty" by A. E. Housman. From "A Shropshire Lad" (Authorized Edition), from *The Collected Poems of A. E. Housman.* Copyright 1939, 1940, © 1965 by Holt, Rinehart and Winston, Inc. Copyright © 1967, 1968 by Robert E. Symons. Reprinted by permission of Holt, Rinehart and Winston, Inc.; The Society of Authors as the literary representative of the Estate of A. E. Housman; and Jonathan Cape Ltd., publishers of A. E. Housman's *Collected Poems.*

"A Start in Life," from *Iowa Interiors* by Ruth Suckow. Copyright 1926 by Alfred A. Knopf, Inc. Copyright 1954 by Ruth Suckow Nuhn. Reprinted by permission of Holt, Rinehart and Winston, Inc.

"The Bridge" by Nicolai Chukovski. From *Treasury of Russian Short Stories 1900-1966*. Copyright 1968 by Frederick Fell, Inc. Reprinted by permission of the publishers.

"We Wear the Mask," from *The Complete Poems of Paul Laurence Dunbar* by Paul Laurence Dunbar. Reprinted by permission of Dodd, Mead & Company.

"Nathan and David," from *The New English Bible*. © The Delegates of the Oxford University Press and the Syndics of the Cambridge University Press 1961, 1970. Reprinted by permission.

"Bush Boy, Poor Boy" by James Aldridge. Copyright © 1951, by Minneapolis Star and Tribune Co., Inc. Reprinted from the May 1951 issue of *Harper's Magazine* by permission of the author's agent.

"The Brave Man of Golo" by Harold Courlander. From *The King's Drum and Other African Stories*. © 1962 by Harold Courlander. Reprinted by permission of Harcourt Brace Jovanovich, Inc.

"Fable for When There's No Way Out." Reprinted by permission of Charles Scribner's Sons from *Half Sun Half Sleep* by May Swenson. Copyright © 1967 May Swenson.

"D-Day." Copyright 1971 by Cor W. Barendrecht, from *Display VII.*

"Utopia" by Ralph H. Fox. Copyright 1929 by Scholastic Magazines, Inc. Reprinted by permission of Scholastic Magazines, Inc.

"A Day No Pigs Would Die," from the novel *A Day No Pigs Would Die* by Robert Newton Peck. Reprinted by permission of the author.

"Father and I." Reprinted with the permission of Hill and Wang, a division of Farrar, Straus and Giroux, from *The Marriage Feast* by Pär Lagerkvist, copyright 1954 by Albert Bonniers Förlag. Also reprinted by permission of Albert Bonniers Förlag.

"I've Gotta Be Free," from the Broadway Musical "Golden Rainbow." Music and lyrics by Walter Marks. Copyright 1967 by

Damila Music, Inc., 40 West 55th Street, New York, NY 10019. All Rights Reserved.

"The Distant Drum" by Calvin Hernton. From *New Negro Poets: USA*, Langston Hughes, ed. Used by permission of Indiana University Press.

"Three-Minute Friendships" by Dana Tregilgas. From *Scholastic Scope.* © 1966 by Scholastic Magazines, Inc. Reprinted by permission of Scholastic Magazines, Inc.

"Haiku" by Phyllis Zylstra McGuinness. Used by permission of the author.

"Hard Row" by Glenn Meeter. From the July 1972 issue of *Redbook* magazine. Copyright © 1972 by the McCall Publishing Company. Used by permission of the author and the McCall Publishing Company.

"If." Copyright 1910 by Rudyard Kipling. From *Rudyard Kipling's Verse:* Definitive Edition. Reprinted by permission of Mrs. George Bambridge and Doubleday & Company, Inc. Also from *Rewards and Fairies,* by Rudyard Kipling; reprinted by permission of Mrs. George Bambridge and the Macmillan Company of Canada Limited.

"The Road Not Taken" by Robert Frost. From *The Poetry of Robert Frost*, edited by Edward Connery Lathem. Copyright 1916, © 1969 by Holt, Rinehart and Winston, Inc. Copyright 1944 by Robert Frost. Reprinted by permission of Holt, Rinehart and Winston, Inc.

"There Will Come a Time" (Ecclesiastes 12), from *The New English Bible.* © The Delegates of the Oxford University Press and the Syndics of the Cambridge University Press 1961, 1970. Reprinted by permission.

TO THE STUDENT

Sometimes life gets a little hectic. Tests to study for, music lessons to practice, household chores to finish, a paper route to face—all these tasks can get to you sometimes.

Other times life gets a little boring. The same daily routine keeps repeating itself; there's nothing exciting to stimulate you.

Except for one thing.

Your imagination.

It's your escape route when life gets too hectic or too ordinary.

It's your avenue to the world of make-believe and illusion.

It's your medium for dreaming dreams: dreams of places you would like to be, of things you would like to do, of persons you would like to become.

And sometimes, when dreams end, as all dreams do, you suddenly realize something about yourself or others you had never been aware of before: something about who you are, or what you want to be, or what you need to do, or what people mean to you, or what God means to you.

This book is about people. Some of them will be like you; some will be quite different. But all share with you a world within: the world of imagination, reflection, and of a growing self-awareness.

Enjoy the dreams. And the discoveries!

HENRY J. BARON
Project Director

Dreaming

Dreams

Hold fast to dreams
For if dreams die,
Life is a broken-winged bird
That can not fly.

Hold fast to dreams
For when dreams go,
Life is a barren field
Frozen with snow.

Langston Hughes

Dream Deferred

What happens to a dream deferred?
Does it dry up
Like a raisin in the sun?
Or fester like a sore—
And then run?
Does it stink like rotten meat?
Or crust and sugar over—
Like a syrupy sweet?

Maybe it just sags
Like a heavy load.

Or does it explode?

Langston Hughes

The Secret Life of Bernard Twichett

Margaret Howard

(With apologies to James Thurber)

The big horse reared up as Bernard called to him—"El Diablo!" In a moment Bernard was riding faster than the wind down the lonely road. The moon shone full. Dark clouds raced across the sky. Bernard's red velvet cape blew in the wind. His jewelled guns twinkled. He was going to rescue his own true love, to carry her away with him before it was too late.

Only he wasn't Bernard Twitchett. He was the daring masked Highwayman. He was the hero of the poem Miss Whipsnade, his English teacher, was reading to the class. He was the outlaw men feared and women loved. His great horse galloped up to the house where his lady waited. There she was in the window. She reached out her arms and called—

"Bernard! Bernard Twitchett! Can you tell the class the answer to that question?"

"Uh . . . I didn't quite hear the question, Miss Whipsnade. Could you please repeat it?"

The English class laughed softly. Bernard saw Mike turn and make a face at him.

"Bernard, how many times must I ask you to pay attention in class?"

Miss Whipsnade was angry. Her glasses bounced on the end of her nose. "This really must stop. You receive a zero for today. Since you can't answer my question, I shall ask Gregory instead. Gregory, who is the King in this poem?"

"It's King George of England," said Gregory. "He wanted to arrest the Highwayman."

"They'll never take me alive," thought Bernard. He hunched down in his seat so Miss Whipsnade couldn't glare at him.

"Now class, since the period is almost over, please pass in your homework," said Miss Whipsnade.

Patty, the girl in front of Bernard, turned to take his paper. "Where's yours?"

"What?" said Bernard.

"Your homework, stupid."

"Oh," said Bernard, dropping his pen. "I guess I must have left it at home."

"Again?" asked Patty. "Boy, are you going to get it!"

"Bernard," said Miss Whipsnade, "will you please give us the first answer to the homework?"

Again Bernard was ashamed. But the Highwayman didn't have to do homework! It seemed that Bernard could not do anything right. The bell rang before he could say anything. He was glad. Miss Whipsnade frowned at him as he went out. Bernard thought, "I really must keep my mind on schoolwork."

He was still thinking that in science class. Mr. Driftwood was talking about rocks. Bernard watched Mr. Driftwood. Mr. Driftwood was wearing baggy pants and brown-and-white shoes. Bernard looked out the window. A beautiful shiny new car was stopped at a traffic light. . . .

"Faster, faster!" laughed Patty. She sat in the soft leather seat next to Bernie. He was at the wheel of his red Manta Ray XCL-500. He touched his alligator shoe to the gas pedal and the powerful car roared down the road. People stopped and stared. How lucky could a guy get! A car like that, and a beautiful girl to take riding in it! Bernie smiled as they passed every car on the road. "Bernie, you're wonderful. You're my—"

"Fossil in the rock, Bernard?" said Mr. Driftwood.

"Uh . . . what was that, Mr. Driftwood?"

"Bernard, have your ears been examined lately? I don't think you're hearing very well. Have they?"

"No . . . I mean yes . . . I mean, my ears are O.K. I just didn't understand the question."

"Then I'll say it again," said Mr. Driftwood, very slowly and loudly. "The question is: How would a scientist explain the fossil in this rock?" He held up a rock.

Bernard's mind was a blank. He said nothing. He tried to remember what he had read about fossils. Nothing. Mr. Driftwood said, "Time's up! How about someone who's a little more with it. James?"

Bernard hunched down in his seat and pretended to listen during the rest of the class. "There's no one more with it than Bernie, the sports car driver," he thought. But he really must try not to look out the window.

At least in gym class there were no windows to look out of. Instead Bernard watched the line of boys in front of him, and the long thick rope they had to climb. Mr. Hammerlock was watching each boy and putting a mark in his grade book. Bernard wished he had worn his good gym shorts. The ones he had on were really his brother's. His brother was six inches taller and 25 pounds heavier than Bernard. Bernard felt he would look better in shorts that fit. He watched Alvin climb the ropes. Alvin was very strong. His muscles looked like big hard lumps on his arms and shoulders. As Alvin climbed, the gym faded away. Bernard heard:

"And next, for the United States of America, the amazing Big Bernard Twitchett!" The huge crowd gathered in Olympic Stadium went wild. Then a hush fell over the audience. Bernard, the single greatest athlete in

the United States, walked smoothly out to the center of the field. His muscles pushed against his blue satin uniform. The athletes from other countries turned away. They knew when they were beaten.

With the grace and speed of a panther, Bernard made the longest broad jump in Olympic history. Then he threw the discus further than it had ever been thrown. After that, Bernard leaped over a 20-foot bar and ran the fastest mile in history. His final effort was a clean lift of a 625-pound weight. When he was through, five gold medals hung around his neck. As the band played, the crowd cheered. Beautiful girls fought to touch him. "Later, girls, later," he told them. Television and newspapers pushed in for interviews. "Tell us, sir, how does it feel to be the world's greatest athlete?"

"Please," said Bernard, smiling humbly, "it was really—"

"Your turn, Twitchett! Let's look sharp!" Mr. Hammerlock was shouting at him.

"Let's go! Move it, man!" Someone in back pushed Bernard. He went up to the rope and looked to the ceiling. It was very far from the floor. Suddenly the room began to spin. Bernard reached for the rope but grabbed air instead.

"Hey, Twitchett! Are you O.K.? You look a little sick," yelled Mr. Hammerlock.

"I'm dizzy," said Bernard.

"O.K., you'll have to sit this one out. But next time, look sharp!" He blew his whistle for the next boy.

Bernard went to the side of the gym. His shorts flapped around his legs. "I'm just hungry," he said to himself. "I really need some lunch."

Later he stood in the cafeteria line. He was waiting to eat the gray meat and lumpy mashed potatoes offered that day. Over the noise he heard Patty saying, "This stuff stinks. We should be able to go out to lunch—"

"How would you like your steak?" Bernard asked Patty. The waiter stood ready to take their order. Around them violins played softly. Candles glowed in the red velvet dining room of Bernard's exclusive club. It was called The Debonair Dukes Club. You had to be a millionaire to belong.

"Bring us a bottle of your finest champagne," Bernard told the waiter. He slipped the man a twenty dollar tip.

For this lunch with Patty, Bernard had chosen to wear one of his custom-made Italian silk suits. He had a hundred of them, with shoes to match. His shirt was also custom-made. His cuff links were ruby and diamond dollar signs. In his back pocket was a thick roll of bills, his spending money for the day.

After lunch, Bernard and Patty were flying down to Florida for some beach time before dinner. Then he had to return in his private plane to his penthouse apartment. He was going to accept his award for "Most Handsome Playboy of the Year." Bernard was not only rich, he was—

"Stupid, that's my lunch," said the boy in back of him.

"Oh, sorry," mumbled Bernard. He reached for his own plate. "If there weren't ladies present, I'd have wiped the floor with him," thought Bernard as he paid for his lunch.

"Just a minute, sonny," called the lady at the cash register as he walked away. "You're 12 cents short."

Life for My Child

Life for my child is simple, and is good.
He knows his wish. Yes, but that is not all.
Because I know mine too.
And we both want joy of undeep and unabiding things,
Like kicking over a chair or throwing blocks out of a
  window
Or tipping over an icebox pan
Or snatching down curtains or fingering an electric
  outlet
Or a journey or a friend or an illegal kiss.
No. There is more to it than that.
It is that he has never been afraid.
Rather, he reaches out and lo the chair falls with a
  beautiful crash,
And the blocks fall, down on the people's heads,
And the water comes slooshing sloppily out across the
  floor.
And so forth.
Not that success, for him, is sure, infallible.
But never has he been afraid to reach.
His lesions are legion.
But reaching is his rule.

Gwendolyn Brooks

Browning has said, "A man's reach should exceed his grasp." Do you agree with that?

Is that idea different from the one in this poem?

Ride a Wild Horse

Ride a wild horse
with purple wings
striped yellow and black
except his head
which must be red.

Ride a wild horse
against the sky
hold tight to his wings . . .
Before you die
whatever else you leave undone,
once, ride a wild horse
into the sun.

Hannah Kahn

Can you think of a "wild horse" you would like to ride?

The Skeptic

Don't look;
You might see.
Don't think;
You might learn.
Don't walk;
You might stumble.
Don't run;
You might fall.
Don't try;
You might fail.
Don't live;
You might die.

Ruby Luse

What is a skeptic? Are you one?

Charles

Shirley Jackson

The day my son Laurie started kindergarten he renounced corduroy overalls with bibs and began wearing blue jeans with a belt; I watched him go off the first morning with the older girl next door, seeing clearly that an era of my life was ended, my sweet-voiced nursery-school tot replaced by a long-trousered, swaggering character who forgot to stop at the corner and wave good-bye to me.

He came home the same way, the front door slamming open, his cap on the floor, and the voice suddenly become raucous shouting, “Isn’t anybody here?”

At lunch he spoke insolently to his father, spilled his baby sister’s milk, and remarked that his teacher said we were not to take the name of the Lord in vain.

"How *was* school today?" I asked, elaborately casual.

"All right," he said.

"Did you learn anything?" his father asked.

Laurie regarded his father coldly. "I didn't learn nothing," he said.

"Anything," I said. "Didn't learn anything."

"The teacher spanked a boy, though," Laurie said, addressing his bread and butter. "For being fresh," he added with his mouth full.

"What did he do?" I asked. "Who was it?"

Laurie thought. "It was Charles," he said. "He was fresh. The teacher spanked him and made him stand in the corner. He was awfully fresh."

"What did he do?" I asked again, but Laurie slid off his chair, took a cookie, and left, while his father was still saying, "See here, young man."

The next day Laurie remarked at lunch, as soon as he sat down, "Well, Charles was bad again today." He grinned enormously and said, "Today Charles hit the teacher."

"Good heavens," I said, mindful of the Lord's name, "I suppose he got spanked again?"

"He sure did," Laurie said. "Look up," he said to his father.

"What?" his father said, looking up.

"Look down," Laurie said. "Look at my thumb. Gee, you're dumb." He began to laugh insanely.

"Why did Charles hit the teacher?" I asked quickly.

"Because she tried to make him color with red crayons," Laurie said. "Charles wanted to color with green crayons, so he hit the teacher and she spanked him and said nobody play with Charles but everybody did."

The third day—it was Wednesday of the first week—Charles bounced a seesaw onto the head of a little girl and made her bleed, and the teacher made him stay inside all during recess. Thursday Charles had to stand in a corner during storytime because he kept pounding his feet on the floor. Friday Charles was deprived of blackboard privileges because he threw chalk.

On Saturday I remarked to my husband, "Do you think kindergarten is too unsettling for Laurie? All this toughness and bad grammar, and this Charles boy sounds like such a bad influence."

"It'll be all right," my husband said reassuringly. "Bound to be people like Charles in the world. Might as well meet them now as later."

On Monday Laurie came home late, full of news. "Charles," he shouted as he came up the hill; I was waiting anxiously on the front steps. "Charles," Laurie yelled all the way up the hill, "Charles was bad again."

"Come right in," I said, as soon as he came close enough. "Lunch is waiting."

"You know what Charles did?" he demanded, following me through the door. "Charles yelled so in school they sent a boy in from first grade to tell the teacher she had to make Charles keep quiet, and so Charles had to stay after school. And so all the children stayed to watch him."

"What did he do?" I asked.

"He just sat there," Laurie said, climbing into his chair at the table. "Hi, Pop, y'old dust mop."

"Charles had to stay after school today," I told my husband. "Everyone stayed with him."

"What does this Charles look like?" my husband asked Laurie. "What's his other name?"

"He's bigger than me," Laurie said. "And he doesn't have any rubbers and he doesn't ever wear a jacket."

Monday night was the first Parent-Teachers meeting, and only the fact that the baby had a cold kept me from going; I wanted passionately to meet Charles's mother.

On Tuesday Laurie remarked suddenly, "Our teacher had a friend come see her in school today."

"Charles's mother?" my husband and I asked simultaneously.

"Naaah," Laurie said scornfully. "It was a man who came and made us do exercises; we had to touch our toes. Look." He climbed down from his chair and squatted down and touched his toes. "Like this," he said. He got solemnly back into his chair and said, picking up his fork, "Charles didn't even *do* exercises."

"That's fine," I said heartily. "Didn't Charles want to do exercises?"

"Naaah," Laurie said. "Charles was so fresh to the teacher's friend he wasn't *let* do exercises."

"Fresh again?" I said.

"He kicked the teacher's friend," Laurie said. "The teacher's friend told Charles to touch his toes like I just did, and Charles kicked him."

"What are they going to do about Charles, do you suppose?" Laurie's father asked him.

Laurie shrugged elaborately. "Throw him out of school, I guess," he said.

Wednesday and Thursday were routine; Charles yelled during story hour and hit a boy in the stomach and made him cry. On Friday Charles stayed after school again, and so did all the other children.

With the third week of kindergarten Charles was an institution in our family; the baby was being a Charles when she cried all afternoon; Laurie did a Charles when he filled his wagon full of mud and pulled it through the kitchen; even my husband, when he caught his elbow in the telephone cord and pulled telephone, ash tray, and a bowl of flowers off the table, said, after the first minute, "Looks like Charles."

During the third and fourth weeks it looked like a

reformation in Charles; Laurie reported grimly at lunch on Thursday of the third week, "Charles was so good today the teacher gave him an apple."

"What?" I said, and my husband added warily, "You mean Charles?"

"Charles," Laurie said. "He gave the crayons around and he picked up the books afterward and the teacher said he was her helper."

"What happened?" I asked incredulously.

"He was her helper, that's all," Laurie said, and shrugged.

"Can this be true, about Charles?" I asked my husband that night. "Can something like this happen?"

"Wait and see," my husband said cynically. "When you've got a Charles to deal with, this may mean he's only plotting."

He seemed to be wrong. For over a week Charles was the teacher's helper; each day he handed things out and he picked things up; no one had to stay after school.

"The P.T.A. meeting's next week again," I told my husband one evening. "I'm going to find Charles's mother there."

"Ask her what happened to Charles," my husband said. "I'd like to know."

"I'd like to know myself," I said.

On Friday of that week things were back to normal. "You know what Charles did today?" Laurie demanded at the lunch table, in a voice slightly awed. "He told a little girl to say a word and she said it and the teacher washed her mouth out with soap and Charles laughed."

"What word?" his father asked unwisely, and Laurie said, "I'll have to whisper it to you, it's so bad." He got down off his chair and went around to his father. His father bent his head down and Laurie whispered joyfully. His father's eyes widened.

"Did Charles tell the little girl to say *that?*" he asked respectfully.

"She said it *twice,*" Laurie said. "Charles told her to say it *twice.*"

"What happened to Charles?" my husband asked.

"Nothing," Laurie said. "He was passing out the crayons."

Monday morning Charles abandoned the little girl and said the evil word himself three or four times, getting his mouth washed out with soap each time. He also threw chalk.

My husband came to the door with me that evening as I set out for the P.T.A. meeting. "Invite her over for a cup of tea after the meeting," he said. "I want to get a look at her."

"If only she's there," I said prayerfully.

"She'll be there," my husband said. "I don't see how they could hold a P.T.A. meeting without Charles's mother."

At the meeting I sat restlessly, scanning each comfortable matronly face, trying to determine which one hid the secret of Charles. None of them looked to me haggard enough. No one stood up in the meeting and apologized for the way her son had been acting. No one mentioned Charles.

After the meeting I identified and sought out Laurie's kindergarten teacher. She had a plate with a cup of tea and a piece of chocolate cake; I had a plate with a cup of tea and a piece of marshmallow cake. We maneuvered up to one another cautiously, and smiled.

"I've been so anxious to meet you," I said. "I'm Laurie's mother."

"We're all so interested in Laurie," she said.

"Well, he certainly likes kindergarten," I said. "He talks about it all the time."

"We had a little trouble adjusting, the first week or so," she said primly, "but now he's a fine little helper. With occasional lapses, of course."

"Laurie usually adjusts very quickly," I said. "I suppose this time it's Charles's influence."

"Charles?"

"Yes," I said, laughing, "you must have your hands full in that kindergarten, with Charles."

"Charles?" she said. "We don't have any Charles in the kindergarten."

The ending to this story comes suddenly, ironically. Irony is something happening contrary to what one expects to happen. Can you find hints in the story that suggest the ending?

The Fifty-Yard Dash

William Saroyan

After a certain letter came to me from New York the year I was twelve, I made up my mind to become the most powerful man in my neighborhood. The letter was from my friend Lionel Strongfort. I had clipped a coupon from *Argosy All-Story Magazine,* signed it, placed it in an envelope, and mailed it to him. He had written back promptly, with an enthusiasm bordering on pure delight, saying I was undoubtedly a man of uncommon intelligence, potentially a giant, and—unlike the average run-of-the-mill people of the world who were, in a manner of speaking, dreamwalkers and daydreamers—a person who would some day be somebody.

His opinion of me was very much like my own. It was pleasant, however, to have the opinion so emphatically corroborated, particularly by a man in New York—and a man with the greatest chest expansion in the world. With the letter came several photographic reproductions of Mr. Strongfort wearing nothing but a little bit of leopard skin. He was a tremendous man and claimed that at one time he had been puny. He was loaded all over with muscle and appeared to be somebody who could lift a 1920 Ford roadster and tip it over.

It was an honor to have him for a friend.

The only trouble was—I didn't have the money. I forget how much the exact figure was at the beginning of our acquaintanceship, but I haven't forgotten that it was an amount completely out of the question. While I was eager to be grateful to Mr. Strongfort for his enthusiasm, I didn't seem to be able to find words with which to explain about not having the money, without immediately appearing to be a dreamwalker and a daydreamer myself. So, while waiting from one day to another, looking everywhere for words that would not blight our friendship and degrade me to commonness, I talked the matter over with my uncle Gyko. He was amazed at my curious ambition, but quite pleased. He said the secret of greatness, according to Yoga, was the releasing within one's self of those mysterious vital forces which are in all men.

These strength, he said in English, which he liked to affect when speaking to me, ease from God. I tell you, Aram, eat ease wonderful.

I told him I couldn't begin to become the powerful man I had decided to become until I sent Mr. Strongfort some money.

Mohney! my uncle said with contempt. I tell you, Aram, mohney is nawthing. You cannot bribe God.

Although my uncle Gyko wasn't exactly a puny man, he was certainly not the man Lionel Strongfort was. In a wrestling match I felt certain Mr. Strongfort would get a headlock or a half-nelson or a toe hold on my uncle and either make him give up or squeeze him to death. And then again, on the other hand, I wondered. My uncle was nowhere near as big as Mr. Strongfort, but neither was Mr. Strongfort as dynamically furious as my uncle. It seemed to me that, at best, Mr. Strongfort, in a match with my uncle, would have a great deal of unfamiliar trouble—I mean with the mysterious vital forces that were always getting released in my uncle, so that very often a swift glance from him would make a big man quail and turn away, or, if he had been speaking, stop quickly.

Long before I had discovered words with which to explain to Mr. Strongfort about the money, another letter came from him. It was as cordial as the first, and as a matter of fact, if anything, a little more cordial. I was delighted and ran about, releasing mysterious vital forces, turning handsprings, scrambling up trees, turning somersaults, trying to tip over 1920 Ford roadsters, challenging all comers to wrestle, and in many other ways alarming my relatives and irritating the neighbors.

Not only was Mr. Strongfort not sore at me, he had reduced the cost of the course. Even so, the money necessary was still more than I could get hold of. I was selling papers every day, but *that* money was for bread and stuff like that. For a while I got up very early every morning and went around town looking for a small satchel full of money. During six days of this adventuring I found a nickel and two pennies. I found also a woman's purse containing several foul-smelling cosmetic items, no money, and a slip of paper on which was written in an ignorant hand: Steve Hertwig, 3764 Ventura Avenue.

Three days after the arrival of Mr. Strongfort's second letter, his third letter came. From this time on our correspondence became one-sided. In fact, I didn't write at all. Mr. Strongfort's communications were overpowering and not at all easy to answer, without money. There was, in fact, almost nothing to say.

It was wintertime when the first letter came, and it was then that I made up my mind to become the most powerful man in my neighborhood and ultimately, for all I knew, one of the most powerful men in the world.

The letters from Mr. Strongfort continued to arrive every two or three days all winter and on into springtime. I remember, the day apricots were ripe enough to steal, the arrival of a most charming letter from my friend in New York. Mr. Strongfort had decided, he said, to teach me everything in one fell swoop, or one sweep fall, or something of that sort. At any rate, for three dollars, he said, he would send me all his precious secrets in one envelope and the rest would be up to me, and history.

I took the matter up with my uncle Gyko. I told him about the letter from Mr. Strongfort.

Mohney! he said. Always he wants mohney. I do not like heem.

Anyhow, he had little use for Mr. Strongfort and regarded the man as a charlatan.

He's all right, I told my uncle.

But my uncle became furious, releasing mysterious vital forces, and said, I wheel break hease head, fooling all you leatle keads.

He ain't fooling, I said. He says he'll give me all his secrets for three dollars.

I tell you, Aram, my uncle Gyko said, he does not know any seacrets. He ease a liar.

I don't know, I said. I'd like to try that stuff out.

Eat ease creaminal, my uncle Gyko said, but I wheel geave you tree dollar.

My uncle Gyko gave me the necessary three dollars and I sent them along to Mr. Strongfort. The envelope came from New York, full of Mr. Strongfort's secrets. They were strangely simple. It was all stuff I had known anyhow but had been too lazy to pay any attention to. The idea was to get up early in the morning and for an hour or so to do various kinds of acrobatic exercises, which were illustrated. Also to drink plenty of water, get plenty of fresh air, eat good wholesome food, and keep it up until you were a giant.

I felt a little let down and sent Mr. Strongfort a short polite note saying so. He ignored the note and I never heard from him again. In the meantime, I had been following the rules and growing more powerful every day. When I say *in the meantime* I mean for four days I followed the rules. On the fifth day I decided to sleep instead of getting up and filling the house with noise and getting my grandmother sore. She used to wake up in the darkness of early morning and shout that I was an impractical fool and would never be rich. She would go back to sleep for five minutes, wake up, and then shout that I would never buy and sell for a profit.

She was wasting her breath, though, because I wasn't enjoying the early-morning acrobatics any more than she was. In fact, I was beginning to feel that it was a lot of nonsense, and that my uncle Gyko had been right about Mr. Strongfort in the first place.

So I gave up Mr. Strongfort's program and returned to my own, which was more or less as follows: to take it easy and grow to be the most powerful man in the neighborhood without any trouble or exercise. Which is what I did.

That spring Longfellow School announced that a track meet was to be held, one school to compete against another; *everybody* to participate.

Here, I believed, was my chance. In my opinion I would be first in every event.

Somehow or other, however, continuous meditation on the theme of athletics had the effect of growing into a fury of anticipation that continued all day and all night, so that before the day of the track meet I had run the fifty-yard dash any number of hundreds of times, had jumped the running broad jump, the standing broad jump, and the high jump, and in each event had made my competitors look like weaklings.

The time came at last for me and three other athletes, one of them a Greek, to go to our marks, get set, and go; and I did, in a blind rush of speed which I knew had never before occurred in the history of athletics.

It seemed to me that never before had any living man moved so swiftly. Within myself I ran the fifty yards fifty times before I so much as opened my eyes to find out how far back I had left the other runners. I was very much amazed at what I saw.

Three boys were four yards ahead of me and going away.

It was incredible. It was unbelievable, but it was obviously the truth. There ought to be some mistake, but there wasn't. There they were, ahead of me, going away.

Well, it simply meant that I would have to overtake them, with my eyes open, and win the race. This I proceeded to do. They continued, incredibly, however, to go away, in spite of my intention. I became irritated and decided to put them in their places for the imper-

tinence, and began releasing all the mysterious vital forces within myself that I had. Somehow or other, however, not even this seemed to bring me any closer to them and I felt that in some strange way I was being betrayed. If so, I decided, I would shame my betrayer by winning the race in spite of the betrayal, and once again I threw fresh life and energy into my running. There wasn't a great distance still to go, but I knew I would be able to do it.

Then I knew I wouldn't.

The race was over.

I was last, by ten yards.

Without the slightest hesitation I protested and challenged the runners to another race, same distance, back. They refused to consider the proposal, which proved, I knew, that they were afraid to race me. I told them they knew very well I could beat them.

It was very much the same in all the other events.

When I got home I was in high fever and very angry. I was delirious all night and sick three days. My grandmother took very good care of me and probably was responsible for my not dying.

What is the tone of this story? (Tone is a certain manner the author has in telling the story.) Is it serious? funny? somewhere in between? Try to find expressions that have helped you decide.

Mirror, mirror on the wall . . .

Echo and Narcissus

retold by Edith Hamilton

This was not the only story about the narcissus. There was another, as magical, but quite different. The hero of it was a beautiful lad, whose name was Narcissus. His beauty was so great, all the girls who saw him longed to be his, but he would have none of them. He would pass the loveliest carelessly by, no matter how much she tried to make him look at her. Heartbroken maidens were nothing to him. Even the sad case of the fairest of the nymphs, Echo, did not move him. She was a favorite of Artemis, the goddess of woods and wild creatures, but she came under the displeasure of a still mightier goddess, Hera herself, who was at her usual occupation of trying to discover what Zeus was about. She suspected that he was in love with one of the nymphs and she went to look them over to try to discover which. However, she was immediately diverted from her investigation by Echo's gay chatter. As she listened amused, the others silently stole away and Hera could come to no conclusion as to where Zeus's wandering fancy had alighted. With her usual injustice she turned against Echo. That nymph became another unhappy girl whom Hera punished. The goddess condemned her never to use her tongue again except to repeat what was said to her. "You will always have the last word," Hera said, "but no power to speak first."

This was very hard, but hardest of all when Echo, too, with all the other lovelorn maidens, loved Narcissus. She could follow him, but she could not speak to him. How then could she make a youth who never looked at a girl pay attention to her? One day, however, it seemed her chance had come. He was calling to his companions, "Is anyone here?" and she called back in rapture, "Here—Here." She was still hidden by the trees so that he did not see her, and he shouted, "Come!"—just what she longed to say to him. She answered joyfully, "Come!" and stepped forth from the woods with her arms outstretched. But he turned away in angry disgust. "Not so," he said; "I will die before I give you power over me." All she could say was, humbly, entreatingly, "I give you power over me," but he was gone. She hid her blushes and her shame in a lonely cave, and never could be comforted. Still she lives in places like that, and they say she has so wasted away with longing that only her voice now is left to her.

So Narcissus went on his cruel way, a scorner of love. But at last one of those he wounded prayed a prayer and it was answered by the gods: "May he who loves not others love himself." The great goddess Nemesis, which means righteous anger, undertook to bring this about. As Narcissus bent over a clear pool for a drink and saw there his own reflection, on the moment he fell in love with it. "Now I know," he cried, "what others have suffered from me, for I burn with love of my own self—and yet how can I reach that loveliness I see mirrored in the water? But I cannot leave it. Only death can set me free." And so it happened. He pined away, leaning perpetually over the pool, fixed in one long gaze. Echo was near him, but she could do nothing; only when, dying, he called to his image, "Farewell—

farewell," she could repeat the words as a last good-by to him.

They say that when his spirit crossed the river that encircles the world of the dead, it leaned over the boat to catch a final glimpse of itself in the water.

The nymphs he had scorned were kind to him in death and sought his body to give it burial, but they could not find it. Where it had lain there was blooming a new and lovely flower, and they called it by his name, Narcissus.

Psychologists refer to a certain kind of mental problem as "narcissism." What do you think that is? Do you know people who are somewhat like Narcissus?

Awakening

The man saw the whole thing very clearly: he saw a boy on a bike riding to the rescue of the world, and he laughed, perhaps because it can't be done, perhaps because it must, perhaps because only a small boy can believe it's worth trying to do.

"The Rescue of the Perishing"

Are there some things you can't lick?

The Cement Truck

Laurence Lasky

I recall being on the bus, wishing my shoulder was separated, or that my right arm had been plastered in a cast, and the cast had a dozen names written on it.

"Mr. Kanele," I wanted to say but didn't dare to, "my left ankle is busted." Or, "Mr. Kanele, I can't move my right leg."

A new thought sprang into my mind. I would arrive at that school, walk up to the nearest wall, and bang my head against it ten or twelve times. That way I would at least get a concussion or brain tumor. Or maybe, I could bend my little finger back to my wrist. Mr. Kanele wouldn't send a guy out on the mat with nine fingers.

Yes, he would! He would send a one-legged third grader onto the mat to keep our team from losing without a try. Maybe, I could slash my wrists or slit my throat. That wouldn't work. Nothing would work. Kanele wouldn't accept any excuse I gave him.

Why was I the only guy on the bus changing from rock to jelly? All the rest of the hearty wrestlers were talking or singing or acting funny. How do you account for that? Maybe all wrestlers are idiots. In fact, you have to be an idiot if you're a wrestler. Everybody hates wrestling. Therefore, wrestlers are idiots—including me, for being on this dumb team.

"There's South Rock High, to the left," said one of the wrestlers.

I pressed my nose against the window. There it was, ugly and cruel. The bus kept rolling along. But now I felt each bump kicking my stomach. I could hear it bouncing emptily like a tin can.

Kanele had told me about the guy I was going to wrestle. "He's county champ, Lasky. A tougher wrestler doesn't exist. He knows every single move in the book. And he's strong as a bull. You're in for one, Lasky."

That really encouraged me. We would walk into that school, and there he would be. I'd walk up to him. He'd look at me and say, "You know what? You're the sickest looking little thing I've ever wrestled. I eat guys like you for breakfast."

I would laugh and say back to him, "Don't you think wrestling is a silly sport? I hate wrestling. Too much practice. I'm going to be a doctor when I grow up."

Then he would look at me as if I were a bug. He would shrug his shoulders and say, "That's your problem, buddy." I would watch him stalking off.

By now we were inside the building. Then Kanele walked up to me. He slapped me on the shoulder. "Get ready. Strip down. The weigh-in's in twenty minutes."

"I thought you said the weigh-in wouldn't be till four," I said.

"My, you really are anxious, Lasky," he said, slapping me on the shoulder.

If you are over or under the weight for your wrestling class, you can't wrestle. Unfortunately, I was the right weight. So was my county champ opponent.

County champ seemed too confident. That made me mad. "Buddy," I whispered to myself, "I'm going to beat the daylights out of you."

Yes, I would, before twenty million cheering fans. I was going to get him on the mat, break his leg, and win the gold belt. Everybody would be cheering like crazy.

And Kanele would walk up to me and say, "You did it, Lasky! You did it!" And I would answer, "I couldn't have done it without you, Mr. Kanele." Then I would be mobbed by a hungry band of autograph seekers and photographers. Cameras would be flashing everywhere.

Just before the match, Kanele gave us his usual pep-talk. "Listen, you guys! We've lost nine matches in a row. It's about time we saved a bit of our school's honor. Lasky, you start us off. Give the boys a lift by pinning the county champ. Now come on, run out on that mat."

So I was supposed to pin the county champ. We ran out on the mat trying to look important. We looked like a pack of toy firemen. I really felt stupid.

I remember the mat being soft and squishy. While everybody else was deciding what holds to use or how to win, I was thinking how nice and soft the mat was. I was also thinking of how sick I was. I was sick of Kanele, sick of wrestling, sick of all the idiot wrestlers around me, and sick of worry.

"Listen," I said to myself, "the worst thing that can happen to you is that you'll get pinned right away. So what? It's been done before. Every member of the team has been pinned quickly before. Well, almost every member."

We sat down in our place. Then the other team came running out on the mat. The crowd was unlike our crowds. At home matches, we were used to having eight people looking down from our side—two managers, a cheerleader, two janitors, and three worried mothers. Here there were a thousand screaming idiots clapping their hands. I remember saying, "I've got to get out of here."

The crowd was screaming for our necks. I noticed

that my idiot teammates were not so cheerful anymore. I was frozen.

I was now standing in my corner. Kanele was talking to me, and the county champ was standing in his corner. His coach was talking to him.

"Mr. Kanele," I said, "I think my back is broke."

"What's that, Lasky?"

"Nothing, oh, nothing."

I remember going out there and shaking hands with the champion. I gave him a pleasant smile, but he didn't seem to see it. Then the moron referee tooted his whistle, and the monster was walking toward me.

Thwap. I was on the mat. He was on me like an octopus. First he had my arm. Then my leg. Then my nose was pushed into that soft, squishy mat. It was a pretty, blue-green mat. I wished I could have been rolled up in it and sent bouncing down a hill.

Then I felt a cement truck on my chest. The referee's hand came down, and his whistle blew. All I could see was Kanele. I looked at him. He looked at me. I felt sick. Kanele came toward me. His eyebrows were down. I could see his upper lip twitching. The eyes were fixed, fixed on my eyes. I could not avoid them. It was a terrible sight.

"Well, Lasky," said Kanele, "at least you didn't quit."

He lied. Boy, did he lie.

Would you have done the same if you had been Lasky?

Have you ever been in a situation where you knew you couldn't win? What did you do?

Me

rough tough neat cool rough toug
h neat cool rough tough neat coo
l rough tough neat cool rough to
ugh neat cool rough tough neat c
ool rough tough neat cool rough
tough neat cool rough tough neat
cool rough **insecure** tough neat
cool rough tough neat cool rough
tough neat cool rough tough neat
cool rough tough neat cool rough
tough neat cool rough tough neat
cool rough tough neat cool rough
tough neat cool rough tough neat
cool rough tough neat cool rough

Marian Krell

We Real Cool

The Pool Players.
Seven at the Golden Shovel.

We real cool. We
Left school. We

Lurk late. We
Strike straight. We

Sing sin. We
Thin gin. We

Jazz June. We
Die soon.

Gwendolyn Brooks

Where does this poem divide, if at all?

Do you remember what term is used to describe a sudden change in the expected outcome of a situation?

My Financial Career

Stephen Leacock

When I go into a bank I get rattled. The clerks rattle me; the wickets rattle me; the sight of the money rattles me; everything rattles me.

The moment I cross the threshold of a bank and attempt to transact business there, I become an irresponsible idiot.

I knew this beforehand, but my salary had been raised to fifty dollars a month and I felt that the bank was the only place for it. So I shambled in and looked timidly round at the clerks. I had an idea that a person about to open an account must needs consult the manager. I went up to a wicket marked "Accountant." The accountant was a tall, cool scoundrel. The very sight of him rattled me. My voice was sepulchral.

"Can I see the manager?" I said, and added solemnly, "alone." I don't know why I said "alone."

"Certainly," said the accountant, and fetched him.

The manager was a grave, calm man. I held my fifty-six dollars clutched in a crumpled ball in my pocket.

"Are you the manager?" I asked.

"Yes," he said.

"Can I see you," I asked, "alone?" I didn't want to say "alone" again, but without it the thing seemed self-evident.

The manager looked at me in some alarm. He felt that I had an awful secret to reveal.

"Come in here," he said, and led the way to a private room. He turned the key in the lock.

"We are safe from interruption here," he said; "sit down."

We both sat down and looked at each other. I found no voice to speak.

"You are one of Pinkerton's men, I presume," he said.

He had gathered from my mysterious manner that I was a detective. I knew what he was thinking, and it made me worse.

"No, not from Pinkerton's," I said, seeming to imply that I came from a rival agency. "To tell the truth," I went on, as if I had been prompted to lie about it, "I am not a detective at all. I have come to open an account. I intend to keep all my money in this bank."

The manager looked relieved but still serious; he concluded now that I was a son of Baron Rothschild or a young Gould.

"A large account, I suppose," he said.

"Fairly large," I whispered. "I propose to deposit fifty-six dollars now and fifty dollars a month regularly."

The manager got up and opened the door. He called to the accountant.

"Mr. Montgomery," he said unkindly loud, "this gentleman is opening an account, he will deposit fifty-six dollars. Good morning."

I rose. A big iron door stood open at the side of the room.

"Good morning," I said, and stepped into the safe.

"Come out," said the manager coldly, and showed me the other way.

I went up to the accountant's wicket and poked the ball of money at him with a quick, convulsive movement as if I were doing a conjuring trick.

My face was ghastly pale.

"Here," I said, "deposit it." The tone of the words

seemed to mean, "Let us do this painful thing while the fit is on us."

He took the money and gave it to another clerk. He made me write the sum on a slip and sign my name in a book. I no longer knew what I was doing. The bank swam before my eyes.

"Is it deposited?" I asked, in a hollow, vibrating voice.

"It is," said the accountant.

"Then I want to draw a check."

My idea was to draw out six dollars of it for present use. Someone gave me a checkbook through a wicket and someone else began telling me how to write it out. The people in the bank had the impression that I was an invalid millionaire. I wrote something on the check and thrust it in at the clerk. He looked at it.

"What! Are you drawing it all out again?" he asked in surprise. Then I realized that I had written fifty-six instead of six. I was too far gone to reason now. I had a feeling that it was impossible to explain the thing. All the clerks had stopped writing to look at me.

Reckless with misery, I made a plunge.

"Yes, the whole thing."

"You withdraw your money from the bank?"

"Every cent of it."

"Are you not going to deposit any more?" said the clerk, astonished.

"Never."

An idiot hope struck me that they might think something had insulted me while I was writing the check and that I had changed my mind. I made a wretched attempt to look like a man with a fearfully quick temper.

The clerk prepared to pay the money.

"How will you have it?" he said.

"What?"

"How will you have it?"

"Oh—" I caught his meaning and answered without even trying to think—"in fifties."

"And the six?" he asked dryly.

"In sixes," I said.

He gave it to me and I rushed out. As the big door swung behind me I caught the echo of a roar of laughter that went up to the ceiling of the bank. Since then I bank no more. I keep my money in cash in my trousers pocket and my savings in silver dollars in a sock.

How does the speaker's fear affect his perceptions of the people in the bank?

Have you ever been panicky in a new situation? What did you do?

Abe Lincoln Grows Up

Carl Sandburg

This excerpt from Sandburg's six-volume biography of Abraham Lincoln gives us a glimpse of Lincoln's "education."

When he was eleven years old, Abe Lincoln's young body began to change. The juices and glands began to make a long, tall boy out of him. As the months and years went by, he noticed his lean wrists getting longer, his legs too, and he was now looking over the heads of other boys. Men said, "Land o' Goshen, that boy air a-growin'!"

As he took on more length, they said he was shooting up into the air like green corn in the summer of a good corn year. So he grew. When he reached seventeen years of age, and they measured him, he was six feet, nearly four inches, high, from the bottoms of his moccasins to the top of his skull.

These were years he was handling the ax. Excepting in spring plowing time and the fall fodder pulling, he was handling the ax nearly all the time. The insides of his hands took on callus thick as leather. He cleared openings in the timber, cut logs and puncheons, split firewood, built pigpens.

He learned how to measure with his eye the half-circle swing of the ax so as to nick out the deepest possible chip from off a tree trunk. The trick of swaying his body easily on the hips so as to throw the heaviest possible weight into the blow of the ax—he learned that.

On winter mornings he wiped the frost from the ax handle, sniffed sparkles of air into his lungs, and beat a steady cleaving of blows into a big tree—till it fell—and he sat on the main log and ate his noon dinner of corn bread and fried salt pork—and joked with the gray squirrels that frisked and peeped at him from high forks of nearby walnut trees.

He learned how to make his ax flash and bite into a sugar maple or a sycamore. The outside and the inside look of black walnut and black oak, hickory and jack oak, elm and white oak, sassafras, dogwood, grapevines, sumac—he came on their secrets. He could guess close to the time of the year, to the week of the month, by the way the leaves and branches of trees looked. He sniffed the seasons.

Often he worked alone in the timbers, all day long with only the sound of his own ax, or his own voice speaking to himself, or the crackling and swaying of branches in the wind, and the cries and whirs of animals; of brown and silver-gray squirrels; of partridges, hawks, crows, turkeys, sparrows, and the occasional wildcats.

The tricks and whimsies of the sky, how to read clear skies and cloudy weather; the creeping vines of ivy and wild grape; the recurrence of dogwood blossoms in spring; the ways of snow, rain, drizzle, sleet, the visitors of sky and weather coming and going hour by hour—he

tried to read their secrets; he tried to be friendly with their mystery.

So he grew, to become hard, tough, wiry. The muscle on his bones and the cords, tendons, cross weaves of fiber, and nerve centers—these became instruments to obey his wishes. He found with other men he could lift his own end of a log—and more too. One of the neighbors said he was strong as three men. Another said, "He can sink an ax deeper into wood than any man I ever saw." And another, "If you heard him fellin' trees in a clearin', you would say there was three men at work by the way the trees fell."

He was more than a tough, long, raw-boned boy. He amazed men with his man's lifting power. He put his shoulders under a new-built corncrib one day and walked away with it to where the farmer wanted it. Four men, ready with poles to put under it and carry it, didn't need their poles. He played the same trick with a chicken house; at the new, growing town of Gentryville nearby they said the chicken house weighed six hundred pounds, and only a big boy with a hard backbone could get under it and walk away with it.

So he grew, living in that Pigeon Creek cabin for a home, sleeping in the loft, climbing up at night to a bed just under the roof, where sometimes the snow and the rain drove through the cracks, eating sometimes at a table where the family had only one thing to eat—potatoes. Once at the table, when there were only potatoes, his father spoke a blessing to the Lord for potatoes; the boy murmured, "Those are mighty poor blessings." And Abe made jokes once when company came and Sally Bush Lincoln brought out raw potatoes, gave the visitors a knife apiece, and they all peeled raw potatoes and talked about the crops, politics, religion, gossip.

Days when they had only potatoes to eat didn't come often. Other days in the year they had "yaller-legged chicken" with gravy, and corn dodgers with shortening, and berries and honey. They tasted of bear meat, deer, coon, quail, grouse, prairie turkey, catfish, bass, perch.

Abe knew the sleep that comes after long hours of work outdoors, the feeling of simple food changing into blood and muscle as he worked in those young years clearing timberland for pasture and corn crops, cutting loose the brush, piling it and burning it, splitting rails, pulling the crosscut saw and the whipsaw, driving the shovel plow, harrowing, planting, hoeing, pulling fodder, milking cows, churning butter, helping neighbors at house raisings, logrollings, cornhuskings.

He found he was fast, strong, and keen when he went against other boys in sports. On farms where he worked, he held his own at scuffling, knocking off hats, wrestling. The time came when around Gentryville and Spencer County he was known as the best "rassler" of all, the champion. In jumping, foot racing, throwing the maul, pitching the crowbar, he carried away the decisions against the lads of his own age always, and usually won against those older than himself.

He earned his board, clothes, and lodgings, sometimes working for a neighbor farmer. He watched his father, while helping make cabinets, coffins, cupboards, window frames, doors. Hammers, saws, pegs, cleats, he understood firsthand, also the scythe and the cradle for cutting hay and grain, the corn cutter's knife, the leather piece to protect the hand while shucking corn, and the horse, the dog, the cow, the ox, the hog. He could skin and cure the hides of coon and deer. He lifted the slippery two-hundred-pound hog carcass, head down, holding the hind hocks up for others of the gang to hook, and swung the animal clear of the ground. He learned where to stick a hog in the underside of the neck so as to bleed it to death; how to split it in two and carve out the chops, the parts for sausage-grinding, for hams, for "cracklings."

Farmers called him to butcher for them at thirty-one cents a day—this when he was sixteen and seventeen years old. He could "knock a beef in the head," swing a maul and hit a cow between the eyes, skin the hide, halve and quarter it, carve out the tallow, the steaks, kidneys, liver.

And the hiding places of fresh spring water under the earth crust had to be in his thoughts; he helped at well digging; the wells Tom Lincoln dug went dry one year after another; neighbors said Tom was always digging a well and had his land "honeycombed"; and the boy Abe ran the errands and held the tools for the well digging.

When he was eighteen years old, he could take an ax at the end of the handle and hold it out in a straight horizontal line, easy and steady—he had strong shoulder muscles and steady wrists early in life. He walked thirty-four miles in one day, just on an errand, to please himself, to hear a lawyer make a speech. He could tell his body to do almost impossible things, and the body obeyed.

Growing from boy to man, he was alone a good deal of the time. Days came often when he was by himself all the time except at breakfast and supper hours in the cabin home. In some years more of his time was spent in loneliness than in the company of other people. It happened, too, that this loneliness he knew was not like that of people in cities who can look from a window on streets where faces pass and repass. It was the wilderness loneliness he became acquainted with; solved; filtered through body, eye, and brain; held communion with in his ears, in the temples of his forehead, in the works of his beating heart.

He lived with trees; with the bush wet with shining raindrops; with the burning bush of autumn; with the lone wild duck riding a north wind and crying down on a line north to south, the faces of open sky and weather, the ax which is an individual one-man instrument—these he had for companions, books, friends, talkers, chums of his endless changing soliloquies.

His moccasin feet in the wintertime knew the white spaces of snowdrifts piled in whimsical shapes against timber slopes or blown in levels across the fields of last year's cut cornstalks; in the summertime his bare feet toughened in the gravel of green streams while he laughed back to the chatter of bluejays in the red-haw trees or while he kept his eyes ready in the slough quack grass for the cow snake, the rattler, the copperhead.

He rested between spells of work in the springtime when the upward push of the coming out of the new grass can be heard, and in autumn weeks when the rustle of a single falling leaf lets go a whisper that a listening ear can catch.

He found his life thrown in ways where there was a certain chance for a certain growth. And so he grew. Silence found him; he met silence. In the making of him as he was, the element of silence was immense.

He took shape in a tall, long-armed cornhusker. When rain came in at the chinks of the cabin loft where he slept, soaking through the book Josiah Crawford lent him, he pulled fodder two days to pay for the book, made a clean sweep, till there wasn't a blade left on a cornstalk in the field of Josiah Crawford.

His father was saying the big boy looked as if he had been roughhewn with an ax and needed smoothing with a jack plane. "He was the ganglin'est, awkwardest feller that ever stepped over a ten-rail snake fence; he had t' duck to git through a door; he 'peared to be all j'ints."

His stepmother told him she didn't mind his bringing dirt into the house on his feet; she could scour the floor, but she asked him to keep his head washed or he'd be rubbing the dirt on her nice whitewashed rafters. He put barefoot boys to wading in a mud puddle near the horse trough, picked them up one by one, carried them to the house upside down, and walked their muddy feet across the ceiling. The mother came in, laughed an hour at the foot tracks, told Abe he ought to be spanked—and he cleaned the ceiling so it looked new.

The mother said, "Abe never spoke a cross word to me in his life since we lived together." And she said Abe was truthful; when Tilda Johnston leaped onto Abe's back to give him a scare on a lonely timber path, she brought the big axman to the ground by pulling her hands against his shoulders and pressing her knee into his backbone. The ax blade cut her ankle, and strips from Abe's shirt and Tilda's dress had to be used to stop the blood. By then she was sobbing over what to tell her mother. On Abe's advice she told her mother the whole truth.

As time went by, the stepmother of Abe became one of the rich, silent forces in his life. Besides keeping the floors, pots, pans, kettles, and milk crocks spick and span, weaving, sewing, mending, and managing with sagacity and gumption, she had a massive, bony, human strength backed with an elemental faith in the unspeakable goodness of God. Hard as life was, she was thankful to be alive.

Once she told Abe how her brother Isaac, back in Hardin County, had hot words with a cowardly young man who shot Isaac without warning. The doctors asked Isaac if they could tie him down while they cut his flesh and took out the bullet. He told them he didn't need to be tied down; he put two lead musket balls in between his teeth and ground his teeth on them while the doctors cut a slash nine inches long and one inch deep till they found the bullet and brought it out. Isaac never let out a moan or a whimper; he set his teeth into the musket balls, ground them into flat sheets, and spat them from his mouth when he thanked the doctors.

Sally Bush, the stepmother, was all of a good mother to Abe. If he broke out laughing when others saw nothing to laugh at, she let it pass as a sign of his thoughts working their own way. So far as she was concerned, he had a right to do unaccountable things; since he never lied to her, why not? So she justified him. When Abe's sister, Sarah, married Aaron Grigsby and a year after died with her newborn child, it was Sally Bush who spoke comfort to the eighteen-year-old boy of Nancy Hanks burying his sister and the wraith of a child.

A neighbor woman sized him up by saying, "He could work when he wanted to, but he was no hand to pitch in like killing snakes." John Romine made the remarks: "Abe Lincoln worked for me, but was always reading and thinking. I used to get mad at him for it. I say he was awful lazy. He would laugh and talk—crack his jokes and tell stories all the time; didn't love work half as much as his pay. He said to me one day that his father taught him to work, but he never taught him to love it."

The farm boys in their evenings at Jones's store in Gentryville talked about how Abe Lincoln was always reading, digging into books, stretching out flat on his stomach in front of the fireplace, studying till midnight and past midnight, picking a piece of charcoal to write on the fire shovel, shaving off what he wrote, and then writing more—till midnight and past midnight. The next thing Abe would be reading books between the plow handles, it seemed to them. And once, trying to speak a last word, Dennis Hanks said, "There's suthin' peculiarsome about Abe."

He wanted to learn, to know, to live, to reach out; he wanted to satisfy hungers and thirsts he couldn't tell about, this big boy of the backwoods. And some of what he wanted so much, so deep down, seemed to be in the books. Maybe in books he would find the answers to dark questions pushing around in the pools of his thoughts and the drifts of his mind. He told Dennis and other people, "The things I want to know are in books; my best friend is the man who'll get me a book I ain't read." And sometimes friends answered, "Well, books ain't as plenty as wildcats in these parts o' Indianny."

This was one thing meant by Dennis when he said there was "suthin' peculiarsome" about Abe. It seemed that Abe made the books tell him more than they told other people. All the other farm boys had gone to school and read *The Kentucky Preceptor*, but Abe picked out questions from it, such as, "Who has the most right to complain, the Indian or the Negro?" and Abe would talk about it, up one way and down the other, while they were in the cornfield pulling fodder for the winter. When Abe got hold of a storybook and read about a boat that came near a magnetic rock, and how the magnets in the rock pulled all the nails out of the boat so it went to pieces and the people in the boat found themselves floundering in water, Abe thought it was funny and told it to other people. After Abe read poetry, especially Bobby Burns's poems, Abe began writing rhymes himself. When Abe sat with a girl, with their bare feet in the creek water, and she spoke of the moon rising, he explained to her it was the earth moving and not the moon—the moon only seemed to rise.

John Hanks, who worked in the fields barefooted with Abe, grubbing stumps, plowing, mowing, said, "When Abe and I came back to the house from work, he used to go to the cupboard, snatch a piece of corn bread, sit down, take a book, cock his legs up high as his head, and read. Whenever Abe had a chance in the field while at work, or at the house, he would stop and read." He liked to explain to other people what he was getting from books; explaining an idea to someone else made it clearer to him. The habit was growing on him of reading out loud; words came more real if picked from the silent page of the book and pronounced on the tongue; new balance and values of words stood out if spoken aloud. When writing letters for his father or the neighbors, he read the words out loud as they got written. Before writing a letter he asked questions, such as, "What do you want to say in the letter? How do you want to say it? Are you sure that's the best way to say it? Or do you think we can fix up a better way to say it?"

As he studied his books, his lower lip stuck out; Josiah Crawford noticed it was a habit and joked Abe about the "stuck-out lip." This habit, too, stayed with him.

He wrote in his sum book, or arithmetic, that compound division was "When several numbers of Divers Denominations are given to be divided by 1 common divisor," and worked on the exercise in multiplication—"If 1 foot contains 12 inches I demand how many there are in 126 feet." Thus the schoolboy.

What he got in the schools didn't satisfy him. He went to three different schools in Indiana, besides two in Kentucky—altogether about four months of school. He learned his A B C; how to spell, read, write. And he had been with the other barefoot boys in butternut jeans learning "manners" under the schoolteacher, Andrew Crawford, who had them open a door, walk in, and say "Howdy do?" Yet what he tasted of books in school was only a beginning, only made him hungry and thirsty, shook him with a wanting and a wanting of more and more of what was hidden between the covers of books.

He kept on saying, "The things I want to know are in books; my best friend is the man who'll git me a book I ain't read." He said that to Pitcher, the lawyer over at Rockport, nearly twenty miles away, one fall afternoon, when he walked from Pigeon Creek to Rockport and borrowed a book from Pitcher. Then when fodder-pulling time came a few days later, he shucked corn from early daylight till sundown along with his father and Dennis Hanks and John Hanks; but after supper he read the book till midnight, and at noon he hardly knew the taste of his corn bread because he had the book in front of him. It was a hundred little things like these which made Dennis Hanks say there was "suthin' peculiarsome" about Abe.

Besides reading the family Bible and figuring his way all through the old arithmetic they had at home, he got hold of *Aesop's Fables, The Pilgrim's Progress, Robinson Crusoe,* and Weems's *The Life of Francis Marion.* The book of fables, written or collected thousands of years ago by the Greek slave known as Aesop, sank deep in his mind. As he read through the book a second and third time, he had a feeling there were fables all around him, that everything he touched and handled, everything he saw and learned had a fable wrapped in it somewhere. One fable was about a bundle of sticks and a farmer whose sons were quarreling and fighting.

There was a fable in two sentences which read: "A

coachman, hearing one of the wheels of his coach make a great noise, and perceiving that it was the worst of the four, asked how it came to take such a liberty. The wheel answered that from the beginning of time creaking had always been the privilege of the weak." And there were shrewd, brief incidents of foolery such as this: "A waggish, idle fellow in a country town, being desirous of playing a trick on the simplicity of his neighbors and at the same time putting a little money in his pocket at their cost, advertised that he would on a certain day show a wheel carriage that should be so contrived as to go without horses. By silly curiosity the rustics were taken in, and each succeeding group who came out from the show were ashamed to confess to their neighbors that they had seen nothing but a wheelbarrow."

The style of the Bible, of Aesop's fables, the hearts and minds back of those books, were much in his thoughts. His favorite pages in them he read over and over. Behind such proverbs as "Muzzle not the ox that treadeth out the corn" and "He that ruleth his own spirit is greater than he that taketh a city," there was a music of simple wisdom and a mystery of common everyday life that touched deep spots in him, while out of the fables of the ancient Greek slave he came to see that cats, rats, dogs, horses, plows, hammers, fingers, toes, people—all had fables connected with their lives, characters, places. There was, perhaps, an outside for each thing as it stood alone, while inside of it was its fable.

One book came, entitled *The Life of George Washington,* "with Curious Anecdotes, Equally Honorable to Himself and Exemplary to His Young Countrymen. Embellished with Six Steel Engravings, by M. L. Weems, formerly Rector of Mt. Vernon Parish." It pictured men of passion and proud ignorance in the government of England driving their country into war on the American colonies. It quoted the far-visioned warning of Chatham to the British parliament, "For God's sake, then, my lords, let the way be instantly opened for reconciliation. I say instantly; or it will be too late forever."

The book told of war, as at Saratoga. "Hoarse as a mastiff of true British breed, Lord Balcarras was heard from rank to rank, loud-animating his troops; while on the other hand, fierce as a hungry Bengal tiger, the impetuous Arnold precipitated heroes on the stubborn foe. Shrill and terrible, from rank to rank, resounds the clash of bayonets—frequent and sad the groans of the dying. Pairs on pairs, Britons and Americans, with each his bayonet at his brother's breast, fall forward together faint-shrieking in death, and mingle their smoking blood." Washington, the man, stood out, as when he wrote: "These things so harassed my heart with grief that I solemnly declared to God, if I know myself, I would gladly offer myself a sacrifice to the butchering enemy if I could thereby insure the safety of these my poor distressed countrymen."

The Weems book reached some deep spots in the boy. He asked himself what it meant that men should march, fight, bleed, go cold and hungry for the sake of what they called "freedom."

"Few great men are great in everything," said the book. And there was a cool sap in the passage: "His delight was in that of the manliest sort, which, by stringing the limbs and swelling the muscles, promotes the kindliest flow of blood and spirits. At jumping with a long pole, or heaving heavy weights, for his years he hardly had an equal."

Such book talk was a comfort against the same thing over again, day after day, so many mornings the same kind of water from the same spring, the same fried pork and corn meal to eat, the same drizzles of rain, spring plowing, summer weeds, fall fodder pulling, each coming every year, with the same tired feeling at the end of the day, so many days alone in the woods or the fields or else the same people to talk with, people from whom he had learned all they could teach him. Yet there ran through his head the stories and sayings of other people, the stories and sayings of books, the learning his eyes had caught from books; they were a comfort; they were good to have because they were good by themselves; and they were still better to have because they broke the chill of the lonesome feeling.

He was thankful to the writer of Aesop's fables because that writer stood by him and walked with him, an invisible companion, when he pulled fodder or chopped wood. Books lighted lamps in the dark rooms of his gloomy hours. . . . Well—he would live on; maybe the time would come when he would be free from work for a few weeks, or a few months, with books, and then he would read. . . . Yes, then he would read. . . . Then he would go and get at the proud secrets of his books.

His father—would he be like his father when he grew up? He hoped not. Why should his father knock him off a fence rail when he was asking a neighbor, passing by, a question? Even if it was a smart question, too pert and too quick, it was no way to handle a boy in front of a neighbor. No, he was going to be a man different from his father. The books—his father hated the books. His father talked about "too much eddication"; after readin', writin', 'rithmetic, that was enough, his father said. He, Abe Lincoln, the boy, wanted to know more than the father, Tom Lincoln, wanted to know. Already Abe knew more than his father; he was writing letters for the neighbors; they hunted out the Lincoln farm to get young Abe to find his bottle of ink with blackberry-brier root and copperas in it, and his pen made from a turkey-buzzard feather, and write letters. Abe had a suspicion sometimes his father was a little proud to have a boy that could write letters, and tell about things in books, and outrun and out-wrestle and rough-and-tumble any boy or man in Spencer County. Yes, he would be different from his father; he was already so; it couldn't be helped.

In growing up from boyhood to young manhood, he had survived against lonesome, gnawing monotony and against floods, forest and prairie fires, snakebites, horse kicks, ague, chills, fever, malaria, "milksick."

A comic outline against the sky he was, hiking along the roads of Spencer and other counties in southern Indiana in those years when he read all the books within a fifty-mile circuit of his home. Stretching up on the long legs that ran from his moccasins to the body frame with its long, gangling arms, covered with linsey-woolsey, then the lean neck that carried the head with its surmounting coonskin cap or straw hat—it was, again, a comic outline—yet with a portent in its shadow. His laughing "Howdy," his yarns and drollery, opened the doors of men's hearts.

What particular qualities of Lincoln described in this excerpt do you wish you had? What personal qualities does he seem to lack?

Phaëthon

retold by Edith Hamilton

The palace of the Sun was a radiant place. It shone with gold and gleamed with ivory and sparkled with jewels. Everything without and within flashed and glowed and glittered. It was always high noon there. Shadowy twilight never dimmed the brightness. Darkness and night were unknown. Few among mortals could have long endured that unchanging brilliancy of light, but few had ever found their way thither.

Nevertheless, one day a youth, mortal on his mother's side, dared to approach. Often he had to pause and clear his dazzled eyes, but the errand which had brought him was so urgent that his purpose held fast and he pressed on, up to the palace, through the burnished doors, and into the throne-room where surrounded by a blinding, blazing splendor the Sun-god sat. There the lad was forced to halt. He could bear no more.

Nothing escapes the eyes of the Sun. He saw the boy instantly and looked at him very kindly. "What brought you here?" he asked. "I have come," the other answered boldly, "to find out if you are my father or not. My mother said you were, but the boys at school laugh when I tell them I am your son. They will not believe me. I told my mother and she said I had better go and ask you." Smiling, the Sun took off his crown of burning light so that the lad could look at him without distress. "Come here, Phaëthon," he said. "You are my son. Clymene told you the truth. I expect you will not doubt my word too? But I will give you a proof. Ask anything you want of me and you shall have it. I call the

Styx to be witness to my promise, the river of the oath of the gods."

No doubt Phaëthon had often watched the Sun riding through the heavens and had told himself with a feeling, half awe, half excitement, "It is my father up there." And then he would wonder what it would be like to be in that chariot, guiding the steeds along that dizzy course, giving light to the world. Now at his father's words this wild dream had become possible. Instantly he cried, "I choose to take your place, Father. That is the only thing I want. Just for a day, a single day, let me have your car to drive."

The Sun realized his own folly. Why had he taken that fatal oath and bound himself to give in to anything that happened to enter a boy's rash young head? "Dear lad," he said, "this is the only thing I would have refused you. I know I cannot refuse. I have sworn by the Styx. I must yield if you persist. But I do not believe you will. Listen while I tell you what this is you want. You are Clymene's son as well as mine. You are mortal and no mortal could drive my chariot. Indeed, no god except myself can do that. The ruler of the gods cannot. Consider the road. It rises up from the sea so steeply that the horses can hardly climb it, fresh though they are in the early morning. In midheaven it is so high that even I do not like to look down. Worst of all is the descent, so precipitous that the Sea-gods waiting to receive me wonder how I can avoid falling headlong. To guide the horses, too, is a perpetual struggle. Their fiery spirits grow hotter as they climb and they scarcely suffer my control. What would they do with you?

"Are you fancying that there are all sorts of wonders up there, cities of the gods full of beautiful things? Nothing of the kind. You will have to pass beasts, fierce beasts of prey, and they are all that you will see. The

Bull, the Lion, the Scorpion, the great Crab, each will try to harm you. Be persuaded. Look around you. See all the goods the rich world holds. Choose from them your heart's desire and it shall be yours. If what you want is to be proved, my son, my fears for you are proof enough that I am your father."

But none of all this wise talk meant anything to the boy. A glorious prospect opened before him. He saw himself proudly standing in that wondrous car, his hands triumphantly guiding those steeds which Jove himself could not master. He did not give a thought to the dangers his father detailed. He felt not a quiver of fear, not a doubt of his own powers. At last the Sun gave up trying to dissuade him. It was hopeless, as he saw. Besides, there was no time. The moment for starting was at hand. Already the gates of the east glowed purple, and Dawn had opened her courts full of rosy light. The stars were leaving the sky; even the lingering morning star was dim.

There was need for haste, but all was ready. The seasons, the gatekeepers of Olympus, stood waiting to fling the doors wide. The horses had been bridled and yoked to the car. Proudly and joyously Phaëthon mounted it and they were off. He had made his choice. Whatever came of it he could not change now. Not that he wanted to in that first exhilarating rush through the air, so swift that the East Wind was outstripped and left far behind. The horses' flying feet went through the low-banked clouds near the ocean as through a thin sea mist and then up and up in the clear air, climbing the height of heaven. For a few ecstatic moments Phaëthon felt himself the Lord of the Sky. But suddenly there was a change. The chariot was swinging wildly to and fro; the pace was faster; he had lost control. Not he, but the horses were directing the course. That light weight in the car, those feeble hands clutching the reins, had told them their own driver was not there. They were the masters then. No one else could command them. They left the road and rushed where they chose, up, down, to the right, to the left. They nearly wrecked the chariot against the Scorpion; they brought up short and almost ran into the Crab. By this time the poor charioteer was half fainting with terror, and he let the reins fall.

That was the signal for still more mad and reckless running. The horses soared up to the very top of the sky and then, plunging headlong down, they set the world on fire. The highest mountains were first to burn, Ida and Helicon, where the Muses dwell, Parnassus, and heaven-piercing Olympus. Down their slopes the flame ran to the low-lying valleys and the dark forest lands, until all things everywhere were ablaze. The springs turned into steam; the rivers shrank. It is said that it was then the Nile fled and hid his head, which still is hidden.

In the car Phaëthon, hardly keeping his place there, was wrapped in thick smoke and heat as if from a fiery furnace. He wanted nothing except to have this torment and terror ended. He would have welcomed death. Mother Earth, too, could bear no more. She uttered a great cry which reached up to the gods. Looking down from Olympus they saw that they must act quickly if the world was to be saved. Jove seized his thunderbolt and hurled it at the rash, repentant driver. It struck him dead, shattered the chariot, and made the maddened horses rush down into the sea.

Phaëthon all on fire fell from the car through the air to the earth. The mysterious river Eridanus, which no mortal eyes have ever seen, received him and put out the flames and cooled the body. The naiads, in pity for him, so bold and so young to die, buried him and carved upon the tomb:—

Here Phaëthon lies who drove the Sun-god's car.
Greatly he failed, but he had greatly dared.

His sisters, the Heliades, the daughters of Helios, the Sun, came to his grave to mourn for him. There they were turned into poplar trees, on the bank of the Eridanus,

Where sorrowing they weep into the stream forever.
And each tear as it falls shines in the water
A glistening drop of amber.

How does Phaëthon's experience compare with "Ride a Wild Horse" or "Life for My Child"?

Is there a contradiction in attitudes? If so, which do you think is the more appropriate?

Daedalus

retold by Edith Hamilton

Daedalus was the architect who had contrived the Labyrinth for the Minotaur in Crete, and who showed Ariadne how Theseus could escape from it. When King Minos learned that the Athenians had found their way out, he was convinced that they could have done so only if Daedalus had helped them. Accordingly he imprisoned him and his son Icarus in the Labyrinth, certainly a proof that it was excellently devised since not even the maker of it could discover the exit without a clue. But the great inventor was not at a loss. He told his son,

Escape may be checked by water and land,
But the air and the sky are free,

and he made two pairs of wings for them. They put them on and just before they took flight Daedalus warned Icarus to keep a middle course over the sea. If he flew too high the sun might melt the glue and the wings drop off. However, as stories so often show, what elders say youth disregards. As the two flew lightly and without effort away from Crete the delight of this new and wonderful power went to the boy's head. He soared exultingly up and up, paying no heed to his father's anguished commands. Then he fell. The wings had come off. He dropped into the sea and the waters closed over him. The afflicted father flew safely to Sicily, where he was received kindly by the King.

What is the myth-writer saying with this treatment of youthful ambition? Do you agree?

Sympathy

I know what the caged bird feels, alas!
   When the sun is bright on the upland slopes;
When the wind stirs soft through the springing grass,
And the river flows like a stream of glass;
   When the first bird sings and the first bud opes,
And the faint perfume from its chalice steals—
I know what the caged bird feels!

I know why the caged bird beats his wing
   Till its blood is red on the cruel bars;
For he must fly back to his perch and cling
When he fain would be on the bough a-swing;
   And a pain still throbs in the old, old scars
And they pulse again with a keener sting—
I know why he beats his wing!

I know why the caged bird sings, ah me,
   When his wing is bruised and his bosom sore,
When he beats his bars and would be free;
It is not a carol of joy or glee,
   But a prayer that he sends from his heart's deep core,
But a plea, that upward to Heaven he flings—
I know why the caged bird sings!

Paul Laurence Dunbar

Do *you* know why the caged bird sings?

The Rescue of the Perishing

William Saroyan

In this story, a boy struggles to solve the problems that result after he plunges into the adult world before he is really ready.

There was a chicken hiding under a parked car on Van Ness Avenue, in the heart of town, on the first rainless day after eleven days and nights of storm, after the floods. And three cars farther down the street, there was a small dog hiding under another car.

He'd never have noticed them on his way home from the public library if they hadn't been so upset about something. The chicken, a big hen with mottled black-and-white feathers, was making noises that were for all the world almost human. And the little dog, a common lost dog not more than twice the size of a cat, was whimpering the same way, making almost the same appeal.

He'd passed up the chicken, astonished that it was there at all and half believing it must belong to the owners of the car, and then he came upon the dog.

It was after six, the streets were almost deserted, he was late for supper. He'd been to the library, examining the whole place—not one book, not one shelf of them, but the whole library, looking into one book after another, as if he were in search of something and knew what it was but just couldn't find it.

Whenever he was at the public library and got to searching that way he forgot time and supper and everything else, sometimes feeling glad about his luck, about drawing nearer to what he was looking for, and sometimes feeling miserable, believing his search was hopeless.

One afternoon during the eleven-day storm he rode out to Skaggs Bridge on his bicycle in answer to a radio appeal, riding six miles in heavy rain. There he got on a truck with twenty others, none of them under sixteen. He was twelve, and eager to prove that twelve years are enough to help in a flood. The truck traveled over muddy roads until it came to where the river was nearest flooding over. The men all smoked in the truck, and the boy took a cigarette when it was offered and tried his best to smoke it. He stayed with the men from five in the afternoon until one in the morning, and worked as hard as any of them. He stopped for coffee and sandwiches only when the others did, and together they put up a high bank.

But when the truck got back to the country store at Skaggs Bridge where he'd left his bike, the bike was gone.

He asked the old man at the store about the bike, telling where he'd put it and the kind it was. It was one he'd bought from Paul Saydak, who'd been rebuilding bikes for twenty years, working in the barn behind his house on Oleander Avenue. It was a lean bike, and strong. Paul Saydak had let him have it for $27.50, although Paul had said it was worth $35.

The old man in the store, at half past one in the morning, hardly knew what the boy was talking about, but he understood that the boy's bike had been swiped, and he couldn't help feeling upset about it. He didn't understand the part about Paul Saydak, but he went outside and let the boy point out to him where he had put the bike. Then he told the boy he hadn't been at the store at five in the afternoon, so he hadn't seen the bike at all. He said he would ask about it, though. He went to the driver of the truck and asked him to get the boy home.

The next day the boy took a bus to school, and the next afternoon he hitchhiked to Skaggs Bridge to ask at the store about his bike. But nobody knew what he was talking about, and he himself felt he was making quite a lot of a $27.50 bike in weather like that, the river free in a dozen different places and millions of dollars lost in damages of all kinds. The bike was gone, that's all. And there wasn't a great deal of interest in the fact that it *was* gone, or in the circumstances under which he had given somebody the best chance in the world to take off with it. He'd listened to the radio appeal for help, he'd got on his bike, he'd gone as fast as he could go to where they'd asked him to go, and there somebody had swiped his bike.

"The radio appeal wasn't to *you,*" his father said the night after the bike had been stolen.

"I thought it was," the boy said.

"No," his father said, "it was to *me,* and I didn't go. You might have known they'd steal your bike."

"I didn't think they would."

"Well, they did. And since they did, and since they had no right to, no right even to be *tempted* to steal it—anybody at the store should have taken it inside and put it away somewhere—well, I'm going to buy you a new bike. Any kind you want. Any time you want it. Tomorrow. You pick it out and I'll buy it."

"That's not it," the boy said. "I don't want a new bike."

"Well, you've lost the old one," the man said. "Pick out the one you want and I'll buy it."

"I liked my bike because I'd bought it with money I'd earned myself," the boy said. He was a little angry with his father for being so angry with whoever had stolen the bike, and with people in general. He knew his father was sympathetic and *did* want him to have a bike, but he didn't like to see his father so angry about people and things in general. The angrier his father got with people, the kinder he became with his family.

"Perhaps it's just as well," his mother said to his father. "So few boys nowadays ride bikes to school, and motorists are so careless. Perhaps it's just as well he's had it stolen. It's always made me worry. Must you have another bike?"

"Of course he must," his father said.

"No," the boy said, "I think I'd rather not have one."

"I'm sure he doesn't want a new bike," his mother said.

"Oh, *are* you?" his father said. He turned to the boy and said, "I leave it to you. Think about it and let me know."

He rode the bus to school after that. It wasn't half as much fun as riding his bike, but it was all right. He couldn't move as freely as he'd moved for a year—for the year he'd had the bike. And every now and then he forgot that the bike had been stolen, so that when he stepped out of the house or out of school he believed he was on his way to his bike and a quick ride to wherever he was going.

Five days after the bike had been stolen, he took the bus after school and rode to town and went to the public library.

He took the place shelf by shelf, forgetting the bike and his father's anger. He read parts of plays, short stories, novels, travel books, histories, biographies, and philosophy. Everything he read seemed fresh and good and new, but not quite what he wanted, not what he was searching for. He was in the public library for hours, sitting down at last to read a story, not knowing the name of the story or who the writer was, and not stopping until the story came to a description of a meal, making him hungry. He looked at the clock and saw that it was twenty past six. His father would be getting home in a few minutes, and supper would start in half an hour. He left the book open on the table and hurried out of the library to the street. The sky was clear and the air seemed clean and fresh, as if nobody had ever breathed it. If he waited for a bus, he might not get home any sooner than if he walked, so he decided to cut through town and enjoy a swift glance at anything he came to, and then get on home. It was a walk of about a mile and a half, but he felt like walking.

When he heard the chicken under the parked car on Van Ness Avenue, he couldn't imagine what it was that was making such a sorrowful appeal for help. Every day the paper was full of stories about strange things that had happened during the storm, so he felt the noise had something to do with it, too. But he didn't expect it to be a chicken, and he didn't expect it to be under a car.

He was some time finding out what it was and where it was, and when he saw that it *was* a chicken under a car he didn't feel that he ought to try to do something for it. It might just belong to the people who owned the car, and they might think he was stealing it. But when he came to the whimpering dog, he knew it belonged to no one, and he was sure he couldn't just leave it there. He called to the dog, but the dog was afraid of him. It took a good three or four minutes to stop the dog from being afraid. The dog crawled out from under the car, still struggling with its fear. The boy was very gentle with the dog, speaking softly and not touching it for some time. At last he began to stroke the dog's head. The dog got to its feet and barked, but all it could manage was one little sound that was more like a cough than a bark.

He picked it up and walked back to where the chicken was.

He set the dog down on the pavement and said, "Now, you just stand there. I'm going to take you home and give you some food and a warm place to sleep, but I've got to get this chicken, too."

The dog watched him and listened to his voice, but couldn't stand still and couldn't understand. It managed to bark again once. It ran off a little, whimpering, and then came back and asked if the boy wanted it to go away.

"Now, will you just stand there a minute while I see about the chicken?" the boy said. "There's a lost chicken under the car here that I've got to take home and take care of, too."

The dog seemed to understand a little, so the boy went around to the back of the car where the hen was sitting as if it were hatching. He began to talk to it, but a bird is a bird, even if it's a hen, and a bird, even if it's lost and sick, has *got* to be afraid of a human being. The hen got to its feet, but not all the way up: not because there wasn't room enough under the car, but because in fear all creatures, even men, do not rise to their full height: only in pride or exultation do they stand very tall, as men do when they are glad about themselves, and then, half dying with joy, crow about who they are and what they can do. The lost hen wobbled to the next car, and then to a third car, the boy going after it slowly and speaking to it softly. He had to crawl under the third car to reach the hen and bring it out.

When the dog saw the hen it began to dance, growling softly—partly, perhaps, because it was a dog and the bird was a bird, and partly, perhaps, because another lost creature had been rescued.

"All right," the boy said to both of them. "Now we're going home."

The dog stayed close to the boy's heels, barking now and then, and the hen stopped being frightened. When the boy got home he picked up the dog and went in through the back door.

He stepped into the dining room, the dog under one arm, the chicken under the other, the eyes of both creatures open and unsure. Everybody at the table stared at the boy, the dog, and the hen.

"I found them," the boy said. "They were hiding under cars on Van Ness. They were both crying. I thought I'd better bring them home."

"Orphans of the storm, is that it?" the father said. "That's not a bad-looking dog."

"Can I keep them?" the boy asked.

"A dog and a chicken?" the mother said.

"They won't be any trouble," the boy said. "I'll fix up a small coop with a nest and a perch for the hen, and the dog can sleep in a box in the garage. Can I keep them?"

"Can he?" his father asked his mother.

"Can he?" the boy's kid brothers asked.

"Well," his mother said, "are you sure you *want* to? I mean, nobody keeps chickens in their yards any more, and dogs—*some* dogs—have a way of getting the people who own them into a lot of trouble."

"I'd like to keep them," the boy said. "They were lost. Nobody wanted them. I found them. They were afraid of me. I had to talk to them. It wasn't easy, especially the hen. I didn't buy them, but I do feel they are mine, and I'd like to keep them."

"Well," his mother said. She turned to his father. "Are you sure it's all right?"

"I don't know why not," his father said.

"All right," his mother said. She got up. "I'll help you put them away until after you've had your supper."

"No," the boy said, "you go ahead. They're both hungry. I'll give the dog a little warm milk to start, and the hen maybe a little rice or something. I won't be a minute."

All the same, his mother went with him to the kitchen and warmed milk for the dog. The boy set the chicken on the floor, and his mother sprinkled rice in front of it, and soon both creatures began to eat and come alive in earnest.

After supper, the boy went to the garage with his younger brothers, and they fixed the hen a small coop with a perch and a nest, and the dog a little house, made out of a small box, with rags on the bottom for a bed.

While they were out in the garage, the boy's father and mother sat in the living room and talked.

"Well, so far he's said nothing about a new bike," the man said. "That bike meant everything in the world to him. You know it did."

"Yes," the woman said, "but *that* bike only. *His* bike. The bike bought with his own money. No other bike can take its place. Something else has got to."

"A stray dog and a tired old hen?" the man said.

"Well, yes," the woman said. "They're *his.* I don't think he'll ever have another bike. I don't think he'll ever want another one. The next time he saves up some money, he'll buy something else. But he did love his bike. It became part of him. He knows it's gone forever, though."

"Then I shouldn't surprise him and bring home a new one?" the man said.

"No," the woman said. "He wouldn't like it. Not *really.* Oh, he'd like it, of course, but it couldn't possibly be what his own bike was."

"Yes, I suppose so," the man said. "Well, it was quite a storm at that, wasn't it?"

"Yes," the woman said. "Everybody's talked of nothing else."

"I can't imagine," the man said, "why you allowed him to ride his bike all the way to Skaggs Bridge in the first place."

"Can you imagine my asking him *not* to?" the woman said. "He *wanted* to. It seemed silly, of course, but it wasn't silly to him, and he *did* help. I mean he did actually do the same work as everybody else."

The man saw the whole thing very clearly: he saw a boy on a bike riding to the rescue of the world, and he laughed, perhaps because it can't be done, perhaps because it must, perhaps because only a small boy can believe it's worth trying to do.

The woman laughed, too, and then both of them stopped quickly, to resume their expressions of earnestness, for they heard him down the hall with his kid brothers, all of them on their way to the living room, to report on what they had done in the brave business of rescuing the perishing.

Why wouldn't a new bike be as good as the old one?

Why did this boy feel that the radio appeal for help was meant for him?

What are the things in your life to which you have strong attachments?

The Summer of Truth

Lucile Vaughan Payne

Whenever I think about last summer, I think of Sammy Trout and the horses, up there in the mountains. And of the gold ring Sammy gave me, and the way we talked about everything. In my own mind, sometimes, I call it the "summer of truth."

It started just after my sophomore year at Nehasset High School—Nehasset is this small Oregon town where Mom and I live. I guess that year was about the worst of my life. I didn't have any friends at all at school. Not one. I don't think Mom realizes that, even to this day, but it's the truth.

Sometimes I think the most important thing in the world to Mom was for me to be popular. She really wanted me to have a lot of friends. The right kind of friends. She kept telling me how important it was to get into the right crowd in high school. At Nehasset, that was Debbie Stone's crowd, and everybody knew it. All the rich kids and popular kids were in it, but Debbie was the real leader. If she liked you, you were in. Or you could get in by dating the right boys, like Scott Williams. I used to spend hours and hours on my clothes and hair and make-up, hoping Scott Williams would notice me. He never did. And Debbie just sort of ignored me.

I did everything I could think of to break in. I hated myself for the things I did, but I couldn't seem to stop. I hung around Debbie's crowd all the time. I pretended to everybody, especially Mom, that I belonged. I followed Scott around. I flattered Debbie until it made me sick. I copied her—the kind of clothes she wore, the way she talked, everything. I even tried to make the other kids think she was a close friend. It was awful. I went around smiling all the time. But I was so tense and unhappy that sometimes I really wanted to die.

Debbie spoke to me, of course. But she spoke to everybody. Even when she saw somebody she didn't know very well, she would smile and say, "Hello there!" So she wasn't unfriendly, I guess. But have you ever had a close friend speak to you like that? Of course not. I used to duck out of sight to keep from meeting her because I was so scared she'd say "hello there" and keep right on going.

I had a real thing about it. *Hello there.* Those two words say everything. They say "you're nothing." They say "go away, you're nobody." Last year I could hear those words in my dreams: *hello there, hello there, hello there.* I'd wake up groaning.

Well, you get the picture. It got harder and harder to pretend to Mom that everything was just great. There were times I felt I couldn't face another day at school. My grades were down, and I had headaches all the time. Nobody had asked me to the Prom. How was I going to explain that to Mom? All during spring term I was on the verge of blowing sky-high any minute.

My appendix saved me. I landed in the hospital about three weeks before school ended. And that's where my "summer of truth" really started.

I would lie there in the hospital and look at my hands and think, this is me, Libby Garrett. *Who is Libby Garrett?* And I really didn't know. I had no idea what sort of person I really was, deep inside. I had pretended to be so many different things to so many people that I couldn't find *me.* Sometimes I wondered whether there *was* a me.

The doctor told Mom I needed a summer of complete rest and plenty of fresh air. That's why I finally wound up with Aunt Shaw and Uncle Ed. They have this little farm in the mountains about forty miles from Nehasset. "I hate to send you to that lonely place," Mom said. I know you'll miss all your friends." I almost laughed. Friends? What friends?

The minute I saw the farm in its beautiful little valley, I was sure I had come to the right place. Aunt Shaw gave me a big hug, not saying much. Aunt Shaw is a quiet woman. Quiet the way the mountains are quiet, big and not bothered. She would let me be *me.* Whatever that was. I wanted to find out.

Well, it was wonderful. Aunt Shaw and Uncle Ed let me move in with them. And then they just left me alone. They didn't ignore me and they didn't make a fuss over me. They just made me feel welcome and left the rest to me. I was supposed to be outdoors a lot, so I started exploring. I loved that farm. Before long I was out every day just walking around, looking at things. Or I'd sit on a log somewhere, doing nothing.

I learned that being alone and being lonely were two different things. I was alone, but never lonely the way I had been in Nehasset. I had lots of time to think about the question that had started bothering me in the hospital. What was I like, deep inside myself? It seemed that my real self was buried under a lot of other things. I wanted to get rid of all that extra stuff. I tried to find *me.* I stopped worrying about what I looked like. I even stopped wearing lipstick. For once in my life, I was going to be myself, completely natural.

Then one day I met Sammy Trout. I was walking in the woods when a pine cone hit me on the shoulder. I turned around, and there was Sammy.

Oh, Sammy. Why is it I want to cry when I think of you now?

He had freckles and he was sunburned. His ears stuck

out. Holes in his sneakers. Ragged jeans. A funny, country boy. But a boy. For a minute I felt the old panic: *Do I look okay? Will he like me?* But that was another Libby, and I was through with her. So I just relaxed and looked at him. He had nice eyes and a kind of serious, old-fashioned way about him. He wore some kind of wide gold ring. I noticed it because it was so odd-looking—sort of lumpy and dented.

"Bet you're the girl at Shaw and Ed's place," he said. "I'm Sammy Trout. I live over the ridge yonder."

"You raise horses," I said. I knew about the Trouts. Fine people, but dirt-poor, Uncle Ed said. Nobody could make a living on horses. But the Trouts kept on trying, year after year.

"You like to ride?" Sammy asked me. "Maybe we could ride up to the old gold mine. I could saddle up a horse for you and bring it over."

"Gee. That sounds great. I've never seen a gold mine."

"See this?" He held out his hand to show me the gold ring. "My dad made that ring for me from a gold nugget I found up there when I was about ten years old. Solid gold. It's kind of soft, so I have to be real careful with it."

That funny old ring meant a lot to Sammy. "I know it ain't worth much," he said. "But I wore it so long now I don't feel right without it. Seems like it's part of me."

We were both horse-crazy, I guess. We rode almost every day that summer. Sometimes Sammy would get his chores done very early and we'd ride out before dawn to see the sunrise from the top of the mountain. I was with him almost all the time. It wasn't a romantic deal. We just liked being together, that's all. Everything was so simple with Sammy. I didn't have to pretend anything. No worries about how I should act. No phony talk. I was just me. And the whole world seemed wonderful.

The only thing that scared me was the thought of going back to school in Nehasset. I wasn't sure I could face it again. One day I asked Sammy, "What's your crowd like?"

He didn't even know what I meant. I tried to tell him how it was. "All the kids in Nehasset High have their own special crowd. They stick together all the time, and date each other, and go to parties and dances and stuff."

That was the only time I ever saw Sammy get mad. "I don't care about your good times down there," he said. "If you don't like it here, why don't you just say so?"

I was stunned. "Oh, Sammy," I said. "Sammy, I wouldn't trade this place for the whole town of Nehasset. I wish I could stay here forever. I *hated* Nehasset. I didn't have any friends at all in that school."

He didn't believe me. "I bet you were the most popular girl in the whole town."

"I was *nobody,*" I said. "It was so bad I used to have nightmares about it. There was a girl at school . . . " I told him about Debbie, about those awful *hello there* dreams. "Those two words made me feel like I didn't even exist. Like I was nothing."

His face got quiet. "Yeah," he said. "I guess it would be pretty bad for a good friend to say that."

"I *was* a nothing."

"That's crazy talk," he said.

It wasn't crazy. I had been a kind of imitation girl all through high school. Why should Debbie or anybody else pay attention to me? I tried to explain it to Sammy. I don't know if he understood it, but I told him. He didn't laugh or criticize. He just listened.

He liked me. That was the miracle. He liked me for

myself. All summer, as we rode and talked, the wonder grew.

But the summer was ending. One day, about two weeks before Mom was due to pick me up, Sammy and I were riding up on the ridge above the farm. We stopped and looked down at it. It was a sight so sweet, so shining . . . and I was going away. I felt tears in my eyes. "Oh, Sammy," I said. I reached out and touched his arm.

I tried to say something. But it wouldn't come out. And Sammy just looked at me, deep and straight. For a long time. Then he leaned toward me. And we kissed.

The whole world seemed to stand still. Then the gong sounded from the farm. It was Aunt Shaw's signal that she wanted me at the house. Sammy and I pulled apart. We just couldn't stop looking at each other.

"You're my girl," said Sammy.

The gong rang again. Sammy grinned. "Come on!" he said. He was off, riding across the field like a crazy man. Me, too. I had a singing, laughing feeling inside. I think that's the happiest I've ever been in my life.

I was still kind of dazed when we reached the house. I got off the horse and leaned against it. I felt weak with happiness. Then I saw Mom.

She gave Sammy a funny look. "Run in and get packed right away, Libby. I've got to get back tonight, and I don't want to drive that road after dark."

"But Mom! School doesn't start for two whole weeks!"

But it was all settled. Shopping to do. A dentist appointment. She had plans. Her voice got a little sharp. She kept looking at Sammy. He was just standing there.

"This is Sammy Trout, Mom."

His face was red. He looked at his feet and said nothing. Oh, Sammy, I thought. *Talk.* Be friendly and nice, so she'll see what a wonderful boy you are. But he sort of turned away from us. I knew people like Mom scared him, but I could tell she thought he was just being rude. "Mom, please," I said. "Can't we at least wait until tomorrow?"

"Libby, I told you. We've got to get back tonight."

I felt terrible. I mumbled something about telling Sammy good-bye. She went into the house, telling me to hurry. Sammy and I just stood there. He didn't look at me. "I sure wish you didn't have to go," he said. His voice sounded funny.

I gritted my teeth so I wouldn't cry. "Maybe I can come back pretty soon. For a weekend."

"You won't come back," he said.

"Yes I will. I've got to."

He pulled off his gold ring. "You take this," he said. "It's all I got."

I looked at the ring through a blur.

"Good-bye, Libby," he said. He wanted to kiss me again. I could tell. But not here. I put my arms around the neck of my horse. "Good-bye," I said. "Good-bye, Sammy."

Then he was gone. I didn't want Mom to see me crying. So I stood there for a while, hurting all over. Then I went inside and packed.

I didn't feel like talking much on the way back to Nehasset. "Who was that funny boy?" Mom asked. "Sammy something-or-other."

I touched the ring. "What's so funny about him. I like him." I could feel myself getting tense. "I like him a lot."

She laughed. "Nothing serious, I hope."

I kept touching the ring. "He gave me this."

"Just what does that mean?"

"He wanted me to have it, that's all."

I was glad when she changed the subject. "I had a talk with Debbie Stone's mother the other day. She promised Debbie would call you right away."

"What for?"

"Oh, the girls are getting a club started. A social thing. They'll be having a party to look over everybody and pick out the ones they want. All the members are voted on. Naturally, you'll be asked to join."

Oh, naturally. I almost laughed. How could Mom be so blind? "I'm not interested," I said. I would *not* go through another year like last year.

"Oh, Libby, don't be silly. You'll want to be with your friends."

Debbie called me a few days later to invite me to the party. I thought I might as well go and get it over with. Funny. For once I didn't feel nervous. I just didn't care.

I wore Sammy's gold ring and one of the new dresses Mom had bought me. I'll have to admit I looked pretty good. The first thing Debbie said was, "Gosh, Libby, you look wonderful!" Last year if anybody had said that to me I would have said, "Oh, I don't either. You know I look just terrible," or something silly like that. I just said, "Thanks."

"No kidding, you look great," she said. "What have you been doing all summer?"

"Riding a horse, mostly."

She took me into the big living room. Everybody was talking about things they'd done together that summer. That left me out. The funny thing is, I didn't care. I just listened, feeling relaxed and easy. After my own summer with Sammy, how could I envy any girl in that room? It suddenly struck me how much alike they all were. Everybody was just imitating everybody else, really. The same old talk. The same slang. The same look. I touched the gold ring. They couldn't hurt me.

Afterward I thought well, that's that. I certainly hadn't done anything to make an impression. I honestly didn't care whether they asked me to join their club or not.

But they did ask me. Now that it didn't make any difference, everybody seemed to like me. Before long, Debbie was treating me like an old friend. Scott Williams was calling me for dates. I was going out and having fun. I was *in*.

Well, there's not much to tell after that. I've found out what it's like to be popular, and it's great. I never dreamed I'd have so many friends. I told the other girls about Sammy, little by little. When I told them his father raised horses, they were really impressed.

I didn't exactly say that Sammy was rich or handsome, or anything like that. But when I talked about that summer in the mountains, they got this other picture of it. You know. The fancy horse ranch, the rancher's son. I didn't really lie about anything, except once. That was when Debbie asked me why I didn't invite Sammy down for a school dance.

"I can't," I said. "He's gone east to prep school." I realized how different Sammy was from the picture they had of him, and I . . . well, I lied, that's all. I didn't want them to see him.

It was in October that I missed the ring. I couldn't remember when I'd taken it off, and I didn't have time to look for it. I meant to, but finally I just forgot about it. After all, it wasn't valuable except as a keepsake.

A long time after that, the whole crowd went to a movie one Saturday night. The stores were open and the streets were still crowded when we came out. As we passed the hardware store, somebody touched my arm and said, "Libby?"

It was Sammy Trout. I guess he had come into town with his dad after a load of feed. He had on old cotton pants and a sweater that was too tight. I had forgotten how his ears stuck out. He looked sort of . . . well, pitiful. I am describing him because I want you to understand what happened next. I wanted to spare his feelings. Think how it would have embarrassed him if I had stopped and introduced him to all those dressed-up kids. And of course, Debbie was right there.

I said, "Hello, there," and kept right on walking. That's all. There was just this one awful flash of feeling. At times I still get it in the pit of my stomach. I don't know why. Nobody even noticed what happened. Nobody but Sammy and me.

Maybe he had tried to call me while I was at the movie. Probably he had been waiting there on the street just hoping he'd see me. I kept going over and over it in my mind while I sat in the Hangout with Scott.

Maybe if I went back to the hardware store. . . . I almost got up and ran out. But what could I say if I did find Sammy?

I began to cry. "Hey, Libby," said Scott. "What's the matter?"

I couldn't talk for a minute. Finally I said, "My ring. I've lost my gold ring." I started crying again. It seemed to me that if I could just find the ring, everything would be all right.

"Well, come on, we'll go back for it."

"No," I said. "Never mind." I shivered. "I want to go home."

I found the ring that same night. It was in the pocket of an old coat. And I've got it in a box at home now, safe. Funny, though. I still have this terrible feeling, sometimes, that I've lost something.

Why do you think Libby ignored Sammy when she saw him in town?

All of us want to be "in" the group and, at the same time, true to self. Which side did Libby pick? Was it the right one? What would you have done in the same circumstances?

Absolute-ly

If roads went nowhere
and rain fell dry,
if birds crawled low
and worms flew high,
if faces were flat
and the midday sky
looked always dark
and the sun shone square,
if beauty were costly
and God unfair
if densest earth
were as thin as air,
if clocks went backwards
and grass grew blue
and lions were happiest
in the zoo
and five were the sum
of two and two
would you be me?
might I be you?

How would we *think*
if all sprouts grew down
and the sea churned pink
and the clouds turned brown
and God's face were fixed
in an awful frown?
I'm thankful, I'm thankful
(are you too?)
that grass is green

and sky is blue
and the sun is round
and fact is true
and we can count on
gravity,
and God is good
and beauty free
and, for the sake of
our sanity,
that you are you
and I am me.

Luci Shaw

Are you thankful too for the things listed here? Are there other "absolutes" you're happy about? Why?

He watched his mother, and he never spoke, but at that moment his youth seemed to be over; . . . It seemed to him that this was the first time he had ever looked upon his mother.

"All the Years of Her Life"

The Conversion of Paul

(Acts 9:1-22)

1 But Paul, threatening with every breath and eager to
destroy every Christian, went to the High Priest in
Jerusalem. 2 He requested a letter addressed to syna-
gogues in Damascus, requiring their cooperation in the
persecution of any believers he found there, both men
and women, so that he could bring them in chains to
Jerusalem.

3 As he was nearing Damascus on this mission, suddenly a brilliant light from heaven spotted down upon
him! 4 He fell to the ground and heard a voice saying to
him, "Paul! Paul! Why are you persecuting me?"

5 "Who is speaking, sir?" Paul asked.

And the voice replied, "I am Jesus, the one you are
persecuting! 6 Now get up and go into the city and await
my further instructions."

7 The men with Paul stood speechless with surprise,
for they heard the sound of someone's voice but saw no
one! 8, 9 As Paul picked himself up off the ground, he
found that he was blind. He had to be led into
Damascus and was there three days, blind, going without food and water all that time.

10 Now there was in Damascus a believer named
Ananias. The Lord spoke to him in a vision, calling,
"Ananias!"

"Yes, Lord!" he replied.

11 And the Lord said, "Go over to Straight Street and
find the house of a man named Judas and ask there for
Paul of Tarsus. He is praying to me right now, for 12 I
have shown him a vision of a man named Ananias
coming in and laying his hands on him so that he can see
again!"

13 "But Lord," exclaimed Ananias, "I have heard
about the terrible things this man has done to the
believers in Jerusalem! 14 And we hear that he has arrest
warrants with him from the chief priests, authorizing
him to arrest every believer in Damascus!"

15 But the Lord said, "Go and do what I say. For Paul
is my chosen instrument to take my message to the
nations and before kings, as well as to the people of
Israel. 16 And I will show him how much he must suffer
for me."

17 So Ananias went over and found Paul and laid his
hands on him and said, "Brother Paul, the Lord Jesus,
who appeared to you on the road, has sent me so that
you may be filled with the Holy Spirit and get your
sight back."

18 Instantly (it was as though scales fell from his eyes)
Paul could see, and was immediately baptized. 19 Then
he ate and was strengthened. He stayed with the believers in Damascus for a few days 20 and went at once to
the synagogue to tell everyone there the Good News
about Jesus—that he is indeed the Son of God!

21 All who heard him were amazed. "Isn't this the
same man who persecuted Jesus' followers so bitterly in
Jerusalem?" they asked. "And we understand that he
came here to arrest them all and take them in chains to
the chief priests."

22 Paul became more and more fervent in his preach-
ing, and the Damascus Jews couldn't withstand his
proofs that Jesus was indeed the Christ.

The Living Bible

All the Years of Her Life

Morley Callaghan

They were closing the drugstore, and Alfred Higgins, who had just taken off his white jacket, was putting on his coat and getting ready to go home. The little gray-haired man, Sam Carr, who owned the drugstore, was bending down behind the cash register, and when Alfred Higgins passed him, he looked up and said softly, "Just a moment, Alfred. One moment before you go."

The soft, confident, quiet way in which Sam Carr spoke made Alfred start to button his coat nervously. He felt sure his face was white. Sam Carr usually said, "Good night," brusquely, without looking up. In the six months he had been working in the drugstore Alfred had never heard his employer speak softly like that. His heart began to beat so loud it was hard for him to get his breath. "What is it, Mr. Carr?" he asked.

"Maybe you'd be good enough to take a few things out of your pocket and leave them here before you go," Sam Carr said.

"What things? What are you talking about?"

"You've got a compact and a lipstick and at least two tubes of toothpaste in your pockets, Alfred."

"What do you mean? Do you think I'm crazy?" Alfred blustered. His face got red and he knew he looked fierce with indignation. But Sam Carr, standing by the door with his blue eyes shining bright behind his glasses and his lips moving underneath his gray mustache, only nodded his head a few times, and then Alfred grew very frightened and he didn't know what to say. Slowly he raised his hand and dipped it into his pocket, and with his eyes never meeting Sam Carr's eyes, he took out a blue compact and two tubes of toothpaste and a lipstick, and he laid them one by one on the counter.

"Petty thieving, eh, Alfred?" Sam Carr said. "And maybe you'd be good enough to tell me how long this has been going on."

"This is the first time I ever took anything."

"So now you think you'll tell me a lie, eh? What kind of a sap do I look like, huh? I don't know what goes on in my own store, eh? I tell you you've been doing this pretty steady," Sam Carr said as he went over and stood behind the cash register.

Ever since Alfred had left school he had been getting into trouble wherever he worked. He lived at home with his mother and his father, who was a printer. His two older brothers were married and his sister had got married last year, and it would have been all right for his parents now if Alfred had only been able to keep a job.

While Sam Carr smiled and stroked the side of his face very delicately with the tips of his fingers, Alfred began to feel that familiar terror growing in him that had been in him every time he had got into such trouble.

"I liked you," Sam Carr was saying. "I liked you and would have trusted you, and now look what I got to do." While Alfred watched with his alert, frightened blue eyes, Sam Carr drummed with his fingers on the counter. "I don't like to call a cop in point-blank," he was saying as he looked very worried. "You're a fool, and maybe I should call your father and tell him you're a fool. Maybe I should let them know I'm going to have you locked up."

"My father's not at home. He's a printer. He works nights," Alfred said.

"Who's at home?"

"My mother, I guess."

"Then we'll see what she says." Sam Carr went to the phone and dialed the number. Alfred was not so much ashamed, but there was that deep fright growing in him, and he blurted out arrogantly, like a strong, full-grown man, "Just a minute. You don't need to draw anybody else in. You don't need to tell her." He wanted to sound like a swaggering, big guy who could look after himself, yet the old, childish hope was in him, the longing that someone at home would come and help him. "Yeah, that's right, he's in trouble," Mr. Carr was saying. "Yeah, your boy works for me. You'd better come down in a hurry." And when he was finished Mr. Carr went over to the door and looked out at the street and watched the people passing in the late summer night. "I'll keep my eye out for a cop" was all he said.

Alfred knew how his mother would come rushing in; she would rush in with her eyes blazing, or maybe she would be crying, and she would push him away when he tried to talk to her, and make him feel her dreadful contempt; yet he longed that she might come before Mr. Carr saw the cop on the beat passing the door.

While they waited—and it seemed a long time—they did not speak, and when at last they heard someone tapping on the closed door, Mr. Carr, turning the latch, said crisply, "Come in, Mrs. Higgins." He looked hard-faced and stern.

Mrs. Higgins must have been going to bed when he telephoned, for her hair was tucked in loosely under her hat, and her hand at her throat held her light coat tight across her chest so her dress would not show. She came in, large and plump, with a little smile on her friendly face. Most of the store lights had been turned out and at first she did not see Alfred, who was standing in the shadow at the end of the counter. Yet as soon as she saw him she did not look as Alfred thought she would look: she smiled, her blue eyes never wavered, and with a calmness and dignity that made them forget that her clothes seemed to have been thrown on her, she put out her hand to Mr. Carr and said politely, "I'm Mrs. Higgins. I'm Alfred's mother."

Mr. Carr was a bit embarrassed by her lack of terror and her simplicity, and he hardly knew what to say to her, so she asked, "Is Alfred in trouble?"

"He is. He's been taking things from the store. I caught him red-handed. Little things like compacts and toothpaste and lipsticks. Stuff he can sell easily," the proprietor said.

As she listened Mrs. Higgins looked at Alfred sometimes and nodded her head sadly, and when Sam Carr had finished she said gravely, "Is it so, Alfred?"

"Yes."

"Why have you been doing it?"

"I been spending money, I guess."

"On what?"

"Going around with the guys, I guess," Alfred said.

Mrs. Higgins put out her hand and touched Sam Carr's arm with an understanding gentleness, and speaking as though afraid of disturbing him, she said, "If you would only listen to me before doing anything." Her simple earnestness made her shy; her humility made her falter and look away, but in a moment she was smiling gravely again, and she said with a kind of patient dignity, "What did you intend to do, Mr. Carr?"

"I was going to get a cop. That's what I ought to do."

"Yes, I suppose so. It's not for me to say, because he's my son. Yet I sometimes think a little good advice is the best thing for a boy when he's at a certain period in his life," she said.

Alfred couldn't understand his mother's quiet composure, for if they had been at home and someone had suggested that he was going to be arrested, he knew she would be in a rage and would cry out against him. Yet now she was standing there with that gentle, pleading smile on her face, saying, "I wonder if you don't think it would be better just to let him come home with me. He looks a big fellow, doesn't he? It takes some of them a long time to get any sense," and they both stared at Alfred, who shifted away with a bit of light shining for a moment on his thin face and the tiny pimples over his cheekbone.

But even while he was turning away uneasily Alfred was realizing that Mr. Carr had become aware that his mother was really a fine woman; he knew that Sam Carr was puzzled by his mother, as if he had expected her to come in and plead with him tearfully, and instead he was being made to feel a bit ashamed by her vast tolerance. While there was only the sound of the mother's soft, assured voice in the store, Mr. Carr began to nod his head encouragingly at her. Without being alarmed, while being just large and still and simple and hopeful, she was becoming dominant there in the dimly lit store. "Of course, I don't want to be harsh," Mr. Carr was saying. "I'll tell you what I'll do. I'll just fire him and let it go at that. How's that?" and he got up and shook hands with Mrs. Higgins, bowing low to her in deep respect.

There was such warmth and gratitude in the way she said, "I'll never forget your kindness," that Mr. Carr began to feel warm and genial himself.

"Sorry we had to meet this way," he said. "But I'm glad I got in touch with you. Just wanted to do the right thing, that's all," he said.

"It's better to meet like this than never, isn't it?" she said. Suddenly they clasped hands as if they liked each other, as if they had known each other a long time. "Good night, sir," she said.

"Good night, Mrs. Higgins. I'm truly sorry," he said.

The mother and son walked along the street together, and the mother was taking a long, firm stride as she looked ahead with her stern face full of worry. Alfred was afraid to speak to her, he was afraid of the silence that was between them, so he only looked ahead too, for the excitement and relief were still pretty strong in him; but in a little while, going along like that in silence made him terribly aware of the strength and the sternness in her; he began to wonder what she was thinking of as she stared ahead so grimly; she seemed to have forgotten that he walked beside her; so when they were passing under the Sixth Avenue elevated and the rumble of the train seemed to break the silence, he said in his old, blustering way, "Thank God it turned out like that. I certainly won't get in a jam like that again."

"Be quiet. Don't speak to me. You've disgraced me again and again," she said bitterly.

"That's the last time. That's all I'm saying."

"Have the decency to be quiet," she snapped. They kept on their way, looking straight ahead.

When they were at home and his mother took off her coat, Alfred saw that she was really only half-dressed, and she made him feel afraid again when she said, without even looking at him, "You're a bad lot. God forgive you. It's one thing after another and always has been. Why do you stand there stupidly? Go to bed, why don't you?" When he was going, she said, "I'm going to make myself a cup of tea. Mind, now, not a word about tonight to your father."

While Alfred was undressing in his bedroom, he heard his mother moving around the kitchen. She filled the kettle and put it on the stove. She moved a chair. And as he listened there was no shame in him, just wonder and a kind of admiration of her strength and repose. He could still see Sam Carr nodding his head encouragingly to her; he could hear her talking simply and earnestly, and as he sat on his bed he felt a pride in her strength. "She certainly was smooth," he thought. "Gee, I'd like to tell her she sounded swell."

And at last he got up and went along to the kitchen, and when he was at the door he saw his mother pouring herself a cup of tea. He watched and he didn't move. Her face, as she sat there, was a frightened, broken face utterly unlike the face of a woman who had been so assured a little while ago in the drugstore. When she reached out and lifted the kettle to pour hot water in her cup, her hand trembled and the water splashed on the stove. Leaning back in the chair, she sighed and lifted the cup to her lips, and her lips were groping loosely as if they would never reach the cup. She swallowed the hot tea eagerly, and then she straightened up in relief, though her hands holding the cup still trembled. She looked very old.

It seemed to Alfred that this was the way it had been every time he had been in trouble before, that this trembling had really been in her as she hurried out half-dressed to the drugstore. He understood why she had sat alone in the kitchen the night his young sister had kept repeating doggedly that she was getting married. Now he felt all that his mother had been thinking of as they walked along the street together a little while ago. He watched his mother, and he never spoke, but at that moment his youth seemed to be over; he knew all the years of her life by the way her hand trembled as she raised the cup to her lips. It seemed to him that this was the first time he had ever looked upon his mother.

Family life in the growing-up years has an unforgettable effect on each member of the family. From glimpses in the story, describe your impression of the Higgins family, being sure to include father, mother, sister, and Alfred. What, in your opinion, are the major reasons they have not been a close and happy family?

A seventeenth-century English poet, John Donne, said: "No man is an island, entire of itself." That is, no man can live completely independent of others. Alfred and his mother have not related to each other for years, and each one has suffered pain because of the lack of relationship. If you were Alfred, how might the events of the evening change your outlook on life and your relationship with other people, especially your mother?

When I Was One-and-Twenty

When I was one-and-twenty
   I heard a wise man say,
'Give crowns and pounds and guineas
   But not your heart away;
Give pearls away and rubies
   But keep your fancy free.'
But I was one-and-twenty,
   No use to talk to me.

When I was one-and-twenty
   I heard him say again,
'The heart out of the bosom
   Was never given in vain;
'Tis paid with sighs a plenty
   And sold for endless rue.'
And I am two-and-twenty,
   And oh, 'tis true, 'tis true.

A. E. Housman

What do you suppose giving "your heart away" means? Are there any words in the poem to help you decide?

"Rue" means "grief"; what made "I" agree with the wise man in a year's time?

A Start in Life

Ruth Suckow

Daisy couldn't wait to start her new job. A new chance, prestige, a better home . . .

The Switzers were scurrying around to get Daisy ready by the time that Elmer Kruse should get through in town. They had known all week that Elmer might be in for her any day. But they hadn't done a thing until he appeared. "Oh, it was so rainy today, the roads were so muddy, they hadn't thought he'd get in until maybe next week." It would have been the same any other day.

Mrs. Switzer was trying now at the last moment to get all of Daisy's things into the battered telescope that lay open on the bed. The bed had not "got made"; and just as soon as Daisy was gone, Mrs. Switzer would have to hurry off to the Woodworths' where she was to wash today. Daisy's things were scattered over the dark brown quilt and the rumpled sheet that were dingy and clammy in this damp weather. So was the whole bedroom, with its sloping ceiling and old-fashioned square-paned windows, the commode that they used for a dresser, littered with pin tray, curlers, broken comb, ribbons, smoky lamp, all mixed up together; the door of the closet open, showing the confusion of clothes and shabby shoes. . . . They all slept in this room—Mrs. Switzer and Dwight in the bed, the two girls in the cot against the wall.

"Mammà, I can't find the belt to that plaid dress."

"Oh, ain't it somewheres around? Well, I guess you'll have to let it go. If I come across it I can send it out to you. Someone'll be going past there."

She had meant to get Daisy all mended and "fixed up" before she went out to the country. But somehow . . . oh, there was always so much to see when she came home. Gone all day, washing and cleaning for other people; it didn't leave her much time for her own house.

She was late now. The Woodworths liked to have her get the washing out early so that she could do some cleaning too before she left. But she couldn't help it. She would have to get Daisy off first. She had already had on her wraps ready to go, when Elmer came—her cleaning cap, of a blue faded almost into gray, and the ancient black coat with gathered sleeves that she wore over her work dress when she went out to wash.

"What's become of all your underclothes? They ain't all dirty, are they?"

"They are, too. You didn't wash for us last week, Mamma."

"Well, you'll just have to take along what you've got. Maybe there'll be some way of getting the rest to you."

"They come in every week, don't they?" Daisy demanded.

"Yes, but maybe they won't always be bringing you in." She jammed what she could into the telescope, thinking with her helpless, anxious fatalism that it would have to do somehow.

"Daisy, you get yourself ready now."

"I am ready. Mamma, I want to put on my other ribbon."

"Oh, that's way down in the telescope somewhere. You needn't be so anxious to fix yourself up. This ain't like going visiting."

Daisy stood at the little mirror preening herself—such a homely child, "all Switzer," skinny, with pale sharp eyes set close together and thin, stringy, reddish hair. She was the oldest, and she got the pick of what clothes were given to the Switzers. Goldie and Dwight envied her. She was important in her small world. She was proud of her blue coat that had belonged to Alice Brooker, the town lawyer's daughter. It hung unevenly about her bony knees, and the buttons came down too far. Her mother had tried to make it over for her.

Mrs. Switzer looked at her, troubled, but not knowing how she could tell her all the things she ought to be told. Daisy had never been away before except to go to her Uncle Fred's at Lehigh. She seemed to think that this would be the same. She had so many things to learn. Well, she would find them out soon enough—only too soon. Working for other people—she would learn what that meant. Elmer and Edna Kruse were nice young people. They would mean well enough by Daisy. It was a good chance for her to start in. But it wasn't the same.

Daisy was so proud. She thought it was quite a thing to be "starting in to earn." She thought she could buy herself so much with that dollar and a half a week. The other children stood back watching her, round-eyed and impressed. They wished that they were going away, like Daisy.

They heard a car come splashing through the mud in low.

"There he is back! Have you got your things on? Goldie—go out and tell him she's coming."

"No, me tell him, me!" Dwight shouted jealously.

"Well—both of you tell him. Land! . . ."

She tried hastily to put on the cover of the bulging telescope and to fasten the straps. One of them broke.

"Well, you'll have to take it the way it is."

It was an old thing, hadn't been used since her husband, Mert, had "left off canvassing" before he died. And he had worn it all to pieces.

"Well, I guess you'll have to go now. He won't want

to wait. I'll try and send you out what you ain't got with you." She turned to Daisy. Her face was working. There was nothing else to do, as everyone said. Daisy would have to help, and she might as well learn it now. Only, she hated to see Daisy go off, to have her starting in. She knew what it meant. "Well—you try and work good this summer, so they'll want you to stay. I hope they'll bring you in sometimes."

Daisy's homely little face grew pale with awe, suddenly, at the sight of her mother crying, at something that she dimly sensed in the pressure of her mother's thin strong arms. Her vanity in her new importance was somehow shamed and dampened.

Elmer's big new Buick, mud-splashed but imposing, stood tilted on the uneven road. Mud was thick on the wheels. It was a bad day for driving, with the roads a yellow mass, water lying in all the wheel ruts. This little road that led past these few houses on the outskirts of town, and up over the hill, had a cold rainy loneliness. Elmer sat in the front seat of the Buick, and in the back was a big box of groceries.

"Got room to sit in there?" he asked genially. "I didn't get out, it's so muddy."

"No, don't get out," Mrs. Switzer said hastily. "She can put this right on the floor there in the back." She added, with a timid attempt at courtesy, "Ain't the roads pretty bad out that way?"

"Yes, but farmers get so they don't think so much about the roads."

"I s'pose that's so."

He saw the signs of tears on Mrs. Switzer's face, and they made him anxious to get away. She embraced Daisy hastily again. Daisy climbed over the grocery box and scrunched herself into the seat.

"I guess you'll bring her in with you some time when you're coming," Mrs. Switzer hinted.

"Sure. We'll bring her."

He started the engine. It roared, then half died down as the wheels of the car spun in the thick, wet mud.

In that moment, Daisy had a startled view of home—the small house standing on a rough rise of land, weathered to a dim color that showed dark streaks from the rain; the narrow sloping front porch whose edge had a soaked, gnawed look; the chickens, greyish-black, pecking at the wet ground; their playthings, stones, a wagon, some old pail covers littered about; a soaked, discolored piece of underwear hanging on the line in the back yard. The yard was tussocky and overhung the road with shaggy long grass where the yellow bank was caved in under it. Goldie and Dwight were gazing at her solemnly. She saw her mother's face—a thin, weak, loving face, drawn with neglected weeping, with its reddened eyes and poor teeth . . . in the old coat and heavy shoes and cleaning cap, her work-worn hand with its big knuckles clutching at her coat. She saw the playthings they had used yesterday, and the old swing that hung from one of the trees, the ropes sodden, the seat in crooked. . . .

The car went off, slipping on the wet clay. She waved frantically, suddenly understanding that she was leaving them. They waved at her.

Mrs. Switzer stood there a little while. Then came the harsh rasp of the old black iron pump that stood out under the box-elder tree. She was pumping water to leave for the children before going off to work.

Daisy held on as the car skidded going down the short clay hill. Elmer didn't bother with chains. He was too used to the roads. But her eyes brightened with scared excitement. When they were down, and Elmer slowed up going along the tracks in the deep wet grass that led to the main road, she looked back, holding on her hat with her small scrawny hand.

Just down this little hill—and home was gone. The big car, the feel of her telescope under her feet, the fact that she was going out to the country, changed the looks of everything. She saw it all now.

Dunkels' house stood on one side of the road. A closed-up white house. The windows stared blank and cold between the old shutters. There was a chair with a broken straw seat under the fruit trees. The Dunkels were old Catholic people who seldom went anywhere. In the front yard was a clump of tall pines, the rough brown trunks wet, the green branches, dark and shining, heavy with rain, the ground underneath mournfully sodden and black.

The pasture on the other side. The green grass, lush, wet, and cold, and the outcroppings of limestone that held little pools of rain water in all the tiny holes. Beyond, the low hills gloomy with timber against the lowering sky.

They slid out onto the main road. They bumped over the small wooden bridge above the swollen creek that came from the pasture. Daisy looked down. She saw the little swirls of foam, the long grass that swished with the water, the old rusted tin cans lodged between the rocks.

She sat up straight and important, her thin little face strained with excitement, her sharp eyes taking in everything. The watery mudholes in the road, the little thickets of plum trees, low and wet, in dark interlacings. She held on fiercely, but made no sound when the car skidded.

She felt the grandeur of having a ride. One wet Sunday Mr. Brooker had driven them all home from church, she and Goldie and Dwight packed tightly into the back seat of the car, shut in by the side curtains against which the rain lashed, catching the muddy scent of the roads. Sometimes they could plan to go to town just when Mr. Pattey was going to work in his Ford. Then they would run out and shout eagerly, "Mr. Pattey! Are you going through town?" Sometimes he didn't hear them. Sometimes he said, with a curt good nature, "Well, pile in"; and they all hopped into the truck back. "He says we can go along with him."

She looked at the black wet fields through which little leaves of bright green corn grew in rows, at showery bushes of sumach along the roadside. A gasoline engine pumping water made a loud desolate sound. There were somber-looking cattle in the wet grass, and lonely, thick-foliaged trees growing here and there in the pastures. She felt her telescope on the floor of the car, the box of groceries beside her. She eyed these with a sharp curiosity. There was a fresh pineapple—something the Switzers didn't often get at home. She wondered if Edna would have it for dinner. Maybe she could hint a little to Edna.

She was out in the country. She could no longer see her house even if she wanted to—standing dingy, streaked with rain, in its rough grass on the little hill. A lump came into her throat. She had looked forward to playing with Edna's children. But Goldie and Dwight would play all morning, without her. She was still proud of her being the oldest, of going out with Elmer and Edna; but now there was a forlornness in the pride.

She wished she were in the front seat with Elmer. She didn't see why he hadn't put her there. She would have liked to know who all the people were who lived on these farms; how old Elmer's babies were; and if he and Edna always went into town on Saturday nights. Elmer must have lots of money to buy a car like this. He had a new house on his farm, too, and Mrs. Metzinger had said that it had plumbing. Maybe they would take her along Saturday nights, too. She might hint about that.

When she had gone to visit Uncle Fred, she had had to go on the train. She liked this better. She hoped they had a long way to go. She called out to Elmer:

"Say, how much farther is your place?"

"What's that?" He turned around. "Oh, just down the road a ways. Scared to drive in the mud?"

"No, I ain't scared. I like to drive most any way."

She looked at Elmer's back, the old felt hat crammed down carelessly on his head, the back of his neck with the golden hair on the sunburned skin above the blue of his shirt collar. Strong and easy and slouched a little over the steering wheel that he handled so masterfully. Elmer and Edna were just young folks; but Mrs. Metzinger said that they had more to start with than most young farmers did, and that they were hustlers. Daisy felt that the pride of this belonged to her too, now.

"Here we are!"

"Oh, is this where you folks live?" Daisy cried eagerly.

The house stood back from the road beyond a space of bare yard with a little scattering of grass just starting—small, modern, painted a bright new white and yellow. The barn was new too, a big splendid barn of frescoed brick, with a silo of the same. There were no trees. A raw, desolate wind blew across the back yard as they drove up beside the back door.

Edna had come out on the step. Elmer grinned at her as he took out the box of groceries, and she slightly raised her eyebrows. She said kindly enough:

"Well, you brought Daisy. Hello, Daisy, are you going to stay with us this summer?"

"I guess so," Daisy said importantly. But she suddenly felt a little shy and forlorn as she got out of the car and stood on the bare ground in the chilly wind.

"Yes, I brought her along," Elmer said.

"Are the roads very bad?"

"Kind of bad. Why?"

"Well, I'd like to get over to Mamma's some time today."

"Oh, I guess they aren't too bad for that."

Daisy pricked up her sharp little ears. Another ride. That cheered her.

"Look in the door," Edna said in a low fond voice, motioning with her head.

Two little round blond heads were pressed tightly against the screen door. There was a clamor of "Daddy, Daddy!" Elmer grinned with a half bashful pride as he stood with the box of groceries, raising his eyebrows with mock surprise and demanding: "Who's this? What you shoutin' 'Daddy' for? You don't think Daddy's got anything for you, do you?" He and Edna were going into the kitchen together, until Edna remembered and called back hastily:

"Oh, come in, Daisy!"

Daisy stood a little left out and solitary there in the kitchen as Billy, the older of the babies, climbed frantically over Elmer demanding candy, and the little one toddled smilingly about. Her eyes took in all of it. She was impressed by the shining blue-and-white linoleum, the range with its nickel and enamel, the bright new woodwork. Edna was laughing and scolding at Elmer and the baby. Billy had made his father produce the candy. Daisy's sharp little eyes looked hungrily at the lemon drops until Edna remembered her. "Give Daisy a piece of your candy," she said.

He would not go up to Daisy. She had to come forward and take one of the lemon drops herself. She saw where Edna put the sack, in a dish high in the cupboard. She hoped they would get some more before long.

"My telescope's out there in the car," she reminded them.

"Oh! Elmer, you go and get it and take it up for her," Edna said.

"What?"

"Her valise—or whatever it is—out in the car."

"Oh, sure," Elmer said with a cheerful grin.

"It's kind of an old telescope," Daisy said conversationally. "I guess it's been used a lot. My papa used to have it. The strap broke when Mamma was fastening it this morning. We ain't got any suitcase. I had to take this because it was all there was in the house, and Mamma didn't want to get me a new one."

Edna raised her eyebrows politely. She leaned over and pretended to spat the baby as he came toddling up to her, then rubbed her cheek against his round head with its funny fuzz of hair.

Daisy watched solemnly. "I didn't know both of your children was boys. I thought one of 'em was a girl. That's what there is at home now—one boy and one girl."

"Um-hm," Edna replied absently. "You can go up with Elmer and take off your things, Daisy," she said. "You can stop and unpack your valise now, I guess, if you'd like to. Then you can come down and help me in the kitchen. You know we got you to help me," she reminded.

Daisy, subdued, followed Elmer up the bright new stairs. In the upper hall, two strips of very clean rag rug were laid over the shining yellow of the floor. Elmer had put her telescope in one of the bedrooms.

"There you are!"

She heard him go clattering down the stairs, and then a kind of murmuring and laughing in the kitchen. The back door slammed. She hurried to the window in time to see Elmer go striding off toward the barn.

She looked about her room with intense curiosity. It

too had a bright varnished floor. She had a bed all of her own—a small, old-fashioned bed, left from some old furnishings that had been put in this room that had the pipes and the hotwater tank. She had to see everything, but she had a stealthy look as she tiptoed about, started to open the drawers of the dresser, looked out of her window. She put her coat and hat on the bed. She would rather be down in the kitchen with Edna than unpack her telescope now.

She guessed she would go down where the rest of them were.

Elmer came into the house for dinner. He brought in a cold, muddy, outdoor breath with him. The range was going, but the bright little kitchen seemed chilly, with the white oilcloth on the table, the baby's varnished high chair and his little fat, mottled hands.

Edna made a significant little face at Elmer. Daisy did not see. She was standing back from the stove, where Edna was at work, looking at the baby.

"He can talk pretty good, can't he? Dwight couldn't say anything but 'Mamma' when he was that little."

Edna's back was turned. She said meaningly:

"Now, Elmer's come in to dinner, Daisy; we'll have to hurry. You must help me get on the dinner. You cut bread and get things on the table. You must help, you know. That's what you are supposed to do."

Daisy looked startled, a little scared and resentful. "Well, I don't know where you keep your bread."

"Don't you remember where I told you to put it this morning? Right over in the cabinet, in that big box. You must watch, Daisy, and learn where things are."

Elmer, a little embarrassed at the look that Edna gave him, whistled as he began to wash his hands at the sink.

"How's Daddy's old boy?" he said loudly, giving a poke at the baby's chin.

As Edna passed him, she shook her head, and her lips just formed: "Been like that all morning!"

He grinned comprehendingly. Then both their faces became expressionless.

Daisy had not exactly heard, but she looked from one to the other, silent and dimly wondering. The queer ache that had kept starting all through the morning, under her interest in Edna's things and doings, came over her again. She sensed something in the atmosphere that she had never known before—some queer difference between her position and that of the two babies, a faint notion of what Mamma had meant when she had said that this would not be visiting.

"I guess I'm going to have the toothache again," she said faintly.

No one seemed to hear her.

Edna whisked off the potatoes, drained the water. . . . "You might bring me a dish, Daisy." Daisy searched a long time while Edna turned impatiently and pointed. Edna put the rest of the things on the table herself. Her young, fresh, capable mouth was tightly closed, and she was making certain resolutions.

Daisy stood hesitating in the middle of the room, a scrawny, unappealing little figure. Billy—fat, blond, in funny, dark blue union-alls—was trotting busily about the kitchen. Daisy swooped down upon him and tried to bring him to the table. He set up a howl. Edna turned, looked astonished, severe.

"I was trying to make him come to the table," Daisy explained weakly.

"You scared him. He isn't used to you. He doesn't like it. Don't cry, Billy. The girl didn't mean anything."

"Here, Daddy'll put him in his place," Elmer said hastily.

Billy looked over his father's shoulder at Daisy with resentful blue eyes. She did not understand it, and felt strangely at a loss. She had been left with Goldie and Dwight so often. She had always made Dwight go to the table. She had been the boss.

Edna said in a cool, held-in voice, "Put these things on the table, Daisy."

They sat down. Daisy and the other children had always felt it a great treat to eat away from home instead of at their own scanty, hastily set table. They had hung around Mrs. Metzinger's house at noon hoping to be asked to stay, not offended when told that "it was about time for them to run off now." Her pinched little face had a hungry look as she stared at the potatoes and fried ham and pie. But they did not watch and urge her to have more, as Mrs. Metzinger did, and Mrs. Brooker when she took pity on the Switzers and had them there.

Daisy wanted more pie. But none of them seemed to be taking more, and so she said nothing. She remembered what her mother had said, with now a faint comprehension: "You must remember you're out working for other folks, and it won't be like it is at home."

After dinner, Edna said: "Now you can wash the dishes, Daisy."

She went into the next room with the children. Daisy, as she went hesitatingly about the kitchen alone, could hear Edna's low contented humming as she sat in there rocking, the baby in her lap. The bright kitchen was empty and lonely now. Through the window, Daisy could see the great barn looming up against the rainy sky. She hoped that they would drive to Edna's mother's place soon.

She finished as soon as she could, and went into the dining room, where Edna was sewing on the baby's rompers. Edna went on sewing. Daisy sat down disconsolately. That queer low ache went all through her. She said in a small, dismal voice:

"I guess I got the toothache again."

Edna bit off a thread.

"I had it awful hard a while ago. Mamma come pretty near taking me to the dentist."

"That's too bad," Edna murmured politely. But she offered no other condolence. She gave a secret little smile at the baby asleep on the blanket and a pillow in one corner of the shiny leather davenport.

"Is Elmer going to drive into town tomorrow?"

"Tomorrow? I don't suppose so."

"Mamma couldn't find the belt of my plaid dress and I thought if he was, maybe I could go along and get it. I'd like to have it."

Daisy's mouth drooped at the corners. Her toothache did not seem to matter to anyone. Edna did not seem to want to see that anything was wrong with her. She had expected Edna to be concerned, to mention remedies. But it wasn't toothache, that strange lonesome ache all over her. Maybe she was going to be terribly sick. Mamma wouldn't come home for supper to be told about it.

She saw Mamma's face in that last glimpse of it—drawn with crying and yet trying to smile, under the old cleaning cap, her hand holding her coat together. . . .

Edna glanced quickly at her. The child was so unattractive and unappealing, even in her forlornness. Edna frowned a little, but said kindly:

"Now you might take Billy into the kitchen out of my way, Daisy, and amuse him."

"Well, he cries when I pick him up," Daisy said faintly.

"He won't cry this time. Take him out and help him play with his blocks. You must help me with the children, you know."

"Well, if he'll go with me."

"He'll go with you, won't he, Billy boy? Won't you go with Daisy, sweetheart?"

Billy stared and then nodded. Daisy felt a thrill of comfort as Billy put his little fat hand in hers and trotted into the kitchen beside her. He had the fattest hands, she thought. Edna brought the blocks and put the box down on the floor beside Daisy.

"Now, see if you can amuse him so that I can get my sewing done."

"Shall you and me play blocks, Billy?" Daisy murmured.

He nodded. Then he got hold of the box with one hand, tipped out all the blocks on the floor with a bang and a rattle, and looked at her with a pleased proud smile.

"Oh, no, Billy. You mustn't spill out the blocks. Look, you're too little to play with them. No, now—now wait! Let Daisy show you. Daisy'll build something real nice—shall she?"

He gave a solemn nod of consent.

Daisy set out the blocks on the bright linoleum. She had never had such blocks as these to handle before. Dwight's were only a few old, unmatched, broken ones. Her spirit of leadership came back, and she firmly put away that fat hand of Billy's whenever he meddled with her building. She could make something really wonderful with these blocks.

"No, Billy, you mustn't. See, when Daisy's got it all done, then you can see what the lovely building is."

She put the blocks together with great interest. She knew what she was going to make—it was going to be a new house; no, a new church. Just as she got the walls up, in came that little hand again, and then with a delighted grunt Billy swept the blocks pell-mell about the floor. At the clatter, he sat back, pursing up his mouth to give an ecstatic "Ooh!"

"Oh, Billy—you mustn't, the building wasn't done! Look, you've spoiled it. Now you've got to sit 'way off here while I try to build it over again."

Billy's look of triumph turned to surprise and then to vociferous protest as Daisy picked him up and firmly transplanted him to another corner of the room. He set up a tremendous howl. He had never been set aside like that before. Edna came hurrying out. Daisy looked at Edna for justification, but instinctively on the defensive.

"Billy knocked over the blocks. He spoiled the building."

"Wah! Wah!" Billy gave loud, heartbroken sobs. The tears ran down his fat cheeks, and he held out his arms piteously toward his mother.

"I didn't hurt him," Daisy said, scared.

"Never mind, lover," Edna was crooning. "Of course he can play with his blocks. They're Billy's blocks, Daisy," she said. "He doesn't like to sit and see you put up buildings. He wants to play, too. See, you've made him cry now."

"Do' wanna stay here," Billy wailed.

"Well, come in with Mother then." She picked him up, wiping his tears.

"I didn't hurt him," Daisy protested.

"Well, never mind now. You can pick up the blocks and then sweep the floor, Daisy. You didn't do that when you finished the dishes. Never mind," she was saying to Billy. "Pretty soon Daddy'll come in, and we'll have a nice ride."

Daisy soberly picked up the blocks and got the broom. What had she done to Billy? He had tried to spoil her building. She always made Dwight keep back until she had finished. Of course it was Daisy, the oldest, who should lead and manage. There had been no one to hear her side. Everything was different. She winked back tears as she swept, poorly and carelessly.

Then she brightened up as Elmer came tramping upon the back porch and then through the kitchen.

"Edna!"

"She's in there," Daisy offered.

"Want to go now? What! Is the baby asleep?" he asked blankly.

Edna gave him a warning look and the door was closed.

Daisy listened hard. She swept very softly. She could catch only a little of what they said—"Kind of hate to go off. . . . I know, but if we once start . . . not a thing all day . . . what we got her for. . . ." She had no real comprehension of it. She hurried and put away the broom. She wanted to be sure and be ready to go.

Elmer tramped out, straight past her. She saw from the window that he was backing the car out from the shed. She could hear Edna and Billy upstairs, could hear the baby cry a little as he was wakened. Maybe she ought to go out and get on her wraps, too.

Elmer honked the horn. A moment later Edna came hurrying downstairs, in her hat and coat, and Billy in a knitted cap and red sweater crammed over his union-alls, so that he looked like a little brownie. The baby had his little coat, too.

Edna called out: "Come in and get this boy, Daddy." She did not look at Daisy, but said hurriedly: "We're going for a little ride, Daisy. Have you finished the sweeping? Well, then, you can pick up those pieces in the dining room. We won't be gone so very long. When it's a quarter past five, you start the fire, like I showed you this noon, and slice the potatoes that were left, and the meat. And set the table."

The horn was honked again.

"Yes! Well, we'll be back, Daisy. Come, lover, Daddy's in a hurry."

Daisy stood looking after them. Billy clamored to sit beside his daddy. Edna took the baby from Elmer and put him beside her on the back seat. There was room—half of the big back seat. There wasn't anything, really, to be done at home. That was the worst of it. They just didn't want to take her. They all belonged together. They didn't want to take anyone else along. She was an outsider. They all—even the baby—had a freshened look of expectancy.

The engine roared—they had started; slipping on the mud of the drive, then forging straight ahead, around the turn, out of sight.

She went forlornly into the dining room. The light from the windows was dim now in the rainy, late afternoon. The pink pieces from the baby's rompers were scattered over the gay rug. She got down on her hands and knees, slowly picking them up, sniffing a little. She heard the Big Ben clock in the kitchen ticking loudly.

That dreadful ache submerged her. No one would ask about it, no one would try to comfort her. Before, there had always been Mamma coming home, anxious, scolding sometimes, but worried over them if they didn't feel right, caring about them. Mamma and Goldie and Dwight cared about her—but she was away out in the country, and they were at home. She didn't want to stay here, where she didn't belong. But Mamma had told her that she must begin helping this summer.

Her ugly little mouth contorted into a grimace of weeping. But silent weeping, without any tears; because she already had the cold knowledge that no one would notice or comfort it.

As you were reading the story, with whom did you sympathize most: Daisy, the Kruses, Mrs. Switzer, or the children?

Can you think of ways the author led you to care about one more than another?

The Bridge

Nicolai Chukovski

"I just can't see him going," Gramma said, turning over the potato cake in the pan with a knife. "He's scared of everything."

"He'll go," Aunt Nadya replied from the depths of the kitchen. "He has to go. He'll be better off there."

Gramma sighed loudly. She wasn't at all convinced Kostya would be better off there.

Kostya had heard every word. He stood not far from the open window amid the currant shrubs, quickly picking the berries and shoving them into his mouth. Since it had been decided he would have to go away, Kostya was spending hours at a time in these shrubs, their luxurious, end-of-July growth serving as an excellent hiding place.

He liked to be alone and not have to talk to anyone. Through the branches creeping over the window sill into the shade-filled kitchen, he could see Gramma's hands moving over the kerosene burner, and hear the sizzling of the frying pancakes.

"He's scared of everything . . . everything," Gramma repeated. "He's afraid to buy a stamp in the post office. How'll he go?"

Kostya's mouth was getting sour from the berries. He worked his way out of the shrubbery, found his bicycle on the dark porch, and opened the kitchen door. Aunt Nadya was peeling potatoes—since it was Sunday she hadn't gone to work in the factory but was helping Gramma. The peels coiled like spirals over Aunt Nadya's thick, manlike fingers. Gramma, a squat, little woman, had just turned over another sizzling pancake. She looked up at the boy. Kostya knew that the mountain of potato cakes piled up in a plate at the burner was being baked for him—one more sign that his going away was final.

"I'm going for a little ride," he said glumly, hoisting the small bicycle over his shoulder.

Gramma sighed, stepping heavily from foot to foot. "Go on; have your last ride," Aunt Nadya told him without lifting her face from the potatoes. "You won't be doing it there."

Kostya walked the bicycle through the open wicket and threw his long leg over the frame. The bike, a juvenile size bought a long time ago, had become too small for him. This year he had shot up to almost twice his previous height, though otherwise he remained the same: narrow shoulders, a thin neck with a protruding Adam's apple, and slightly protuberant, translucent ears.

Mechanically Kostya rode out into the alley, hedged by dusty elder thickets. His sharp knees almost touched his chin, but he didn't mind—he was much too used to it. Mechanically he swerved to his left to cut into the open fields; he didn't want to meet anybody and didn't want anybody to disturb his thoughts.

Last spring after he was graduated from high school, barely getting promoted, Kostya had decided that going to the institute was out of the question. There had been a time his marks were no worse than anybody else's, but after his mother had died, a year and a half ago, he hadn't attended school for several months, and he had fallen too far behind to catch up. Everybody in class had known that Kostya never learned his lessons. He had become shy and unsure of himself, and the shyness had compounded his confusion whenever he'd been called to the blackboard.

And then his awkwardness. In company he'd either keep quiet or blurt out anything that came to his mind, then feel ashamed of himself. He had begun to avoid people, went swimming by himself, had even given up the soccer team. Once he had been shortchanged in the bakery shop and instead of reminding the saleswoman that she had made a mistake, he had told his grandmother that he had lost the money. Gramma was the only one with whom he felt at ease, unafraid. But now he'd have to leave her. . . .

This was the third year Gramma hadn't worked in the factory but had lived on her pension. Aunt Nadya had four little children; her husband had gone into construction work somewhere on the Volga, and there were rumors he had himself another woman—for the last year he hadn't sent home a kopeck. The whole settlement where Kostya had been born and lived all his starless seventeen years was made up of people working in the factory. It was a women's factory where a true man wouldn't be caught working.

Lads would leave the settlement as soon as they were graduated, and Kostya, too, would have to leave and stop living at Gramma's and Aunt Nadya's expense. But where? Uncle Vassily Petrovitch, Gramma's brother, had asked him to come, promising Gramma to take good care of him and find him a job. Everybody had thought that this was good and right, that a bright future was ahead of him . . . everybody but Kostya. Deep inside he was afraid nothing would come out of it; yet he didn't dare tell anybody.

He didn't dare confess to anybody how frightening was the thought of leaving Gramma. Uncle Vassily Petrovitch loomed in Kostya's mind like a cold, strict, old man of whom even Gramma was afraid. Quite often she had warned him "not to do anything to spite your uncle." Uncle Vasya had left for Siberia many years ago, before Kostya was even born, when his mother was still a little girl. He had been a tugboat captain on that great Siberian river that flows into the Arctic Ocean, but now he was more than that—he was a chief over a whole fleet of boats. Kostya often saw this river on a large map hanging in the classroom; with all its winding tributaries it reminded him of some strange plant with many weird roots stretching and stretching. . . .

Uncle Vasya often asked that Kostya come. "I'll enter him in the River Technicum together with my son Kolya," he wrote. "They will drill them there so that in three years both of them will become fine navigators."

When Gramma had read that letter she flinched and cast Kostya a frightened look at the word *drill.* And yet tonight they would go to the railroad station and wait for the Moscow train arriving at five in the morning. He would leave all by himself for Moscow, the unfamiliar, big city he had never seen before, and in Moscow he'd have to find his way to another railroad station, board another train leaving for Siberia, and he'd be all by himself with nothing to remind him of Gramma's comfort apart from the potato pancakes in the basket.

It was a warm but sunless, overcast day. Kostya rode out of the settlement and turned onto the highway running amid wavy fields. To the right, about three kilometers away, stretched the river—wide at times, hiding at times behind soft hills. The cloud-covered sky seemed to be hanging low over the usually busy highway, now deserted because it was Sunday. A warm, hay-scented breeze caressed the boy's face, as though careful not to disturb his thinking.

Deep in his thoughts, Kostya pushed the pedals, unaware of a little bird that kept perching on a telegraph post ahead of him, swinging its long tail, and seeming to wait until he caught up with it, then flying up again, perching on another post, farther away, and waiting again. The boy did not notice it, nor the old, thick-leaved linden trees—the remnants of an old road on which this highway was constructed—shooting up here and there like petrified explosions. Kostya pedaled onward where the gray ribbon of the macadam ran into the sunless twilight, rising softly or sloping gently.

Each time Kostya reached a crest of the wavy road, he had an excellent view to the next crest. Each time he was on the top of a hill he could see a green depression through which the road made a straight cut, first running down then up toward the crest where it butted against the sky and disappeared.

Hurdling one of these crests, Kostya sighted in the distance a minute, colored dot moving in the same direction. It occurred to him he might have noticed it before but had paid it no attention. There might have been a two-kilometer span between them—he only had a glimpse of it, looming blue and yellow, before it reached the next crest and vanished.

Kostya began to pedal faster. He dashed downhill, bouncing over a little bridge that spanned the two banks of a gully, then climbed the uphill stretch, using the impetus gained from the down-drive. He hurdled the crest and saw again the yellow-blue dot—bigger now, just beginning to move up the next rise. The distance between them had been shortened considerably; he could see it was somebody on a bicycle. How odd, he thought, so gaily dressed, yellow on top, blue below. Quite intrigued, Kostya leaned forward, pumping harder and harder, trying for greater speed.

As soon as he came over the next crest, he realized that the cyclist ahead of him was a girl wearing a blue skirt and yellow blouse, her fair hair falling down her back. She had been pedaling unhurriedly until she heard him coming from behind. As she turned her face to him, the glimpse Kostya caught was brief—a round, babyish face. There were still about two hundred meters separating them, and when she turned away again, her plump, little calves in the white socks began to push harder—the girl didn't want to be outdistanced.

She spurted ahead. Kostya leaned forward on the bars, pumping with all his might. Yet he was unable to cut the distance by much—she seemed to be quite good. On the next rise he appeared to gain a little, but when they came down the slope and the bikes rolled on their own, he stayed back somewhat. Her bike's better than mine, he thought. Yet the excitement of the chase added will to his strength. On the next rise he gained considerably, and covered the next downhill stretch, long as it was, without giving in a meter. Now he could see her well—no more than thirteen or fourteen. At times the girl turned her head slightly, seeming to try to catch a glimpse of him from the corner of her eye. Then he saw her chubby cheek, and a moment later he'd see her trying desperately to keep him from catching up with her. But he was drawing inexorably closer.

The girl's hair fluttered in the wind, exposing the back of her neck. They sped out of the fields, plunging into a forest of aspen, spruce and birch trees that seemed to rise into a solid wall. As the distance between the bicycles stubbornly decreased, Kostya was overcome by a sense of triumph. The girl's glances were more frequent, every time she tried to have a look at him, her bike made a little zig-zag, and he gained a few meters. He was sure now to catch up with her, probably on the next rise.

A recently laid asphalt road turned off the highway into the forest, right at the start of the rise. Kostya knew where it led—toward the river where a new bridge was being built to connect the state farms on both sides. But what he did not suspect was that the pursued bicycle would turn off to that road.

The girl made the turn abruptly. It was so sudden that he almost flashed by. She might have thought he would follow the highway and stop pursuing her. But Kostya had become so intensely elated that all he could think of now was catching up with her. He, too, swerved from the highway and spurted after her.

The road was downhill all the way. Both bicycles were tearing down at their maximum speeds, the girl steadily about ten meters ahead of Kostya. But he didn't care anymore—the road only led to the bridge now under construction and she'd have no choice but to stop there.

The road approached the bridge at an angle; through the tree trunks at the right the mirror of the river flashed far below under its steep bank. Cement barrels, sifters, and wooden scaffolding loomed before their eyes together with piles upon piles of scrap concrete—the unfinished structure was right in front of them.

The bridgework had no top layer yet, but it spanned both banks. It looked like a net scaled by a formless hodge-podge of wood in which the future metallic slickness could only be vaguely surmised. Now because it was Sunday, instead of the unceasing hum of work, a deep silence stood over the river.

Everything happened so fast that Kostya had no time to consider the danger. Suddenly he saw that the asphalt was coming to an end, and a four-plank trestle, laid over a sand embankment, led to the bridge. The girl pedaled ahead at top speed. Kostya was so shocked that before he had time to recover his wits he found himself, too, bouncing along those planks. He gripped the bar firmly to avoid veering off onto the sand. But the sand wasn't what bothered him. What frightened him was the realization that the trestle ran from the embankment onto the truss, across the unfenced iron girders which served as a narrow path for the bridge workers—high above the water. Was she insane? She was coming to the end of the embankment without slowing down!

"Brake! Brake!" he managed to shout out. But then he choked on his own words.

The girl half-turned at the sound of his voice. Again she glanced at him from the corner of one eye. Her bicycle, making a slight zig-zag, almost pulled her off the planks. But she managed to straighten out the wheel and spurt straight ahead, onto the truss, over the narrow path suspended high above the water.

Something is terribly wrong here, flashed through Kostya's mind. He should have braked short of the bridge but for some uncanny reason he hadn't done so.

His bike carried him onto the truss, onto those same planks, high above the water. . . .

There was no more time to stop, turn or look back. The only way was straight ahead—with no let-up of speed. His hand must not jerk. He knew he couldn't stand the suspense; he'd weaken from fear. But he must go on . . . because of her . . . because her bike was straight ahead. . . .

Kostya couldn't tear his eyes away from the girl. She rode evenly, unswervingly, yet he sensed a desperate tension in that straightness. How can she stand it! Oh, if she only doesn't get it into her head to look back! How far is it to the end of the bridge? If she can only keep her hand from jerking! If only she'll not try to look back! She's over more than half—one more minute, and it'll be all over. Just that she doesn't look back!

The girl did look back.

She turned her head just slightly, just to make sure from the corner of her eye that he was behind. As she turned, her front wheel gave a slight jerk. A second, a long eternity, she struggled with it, trying to make it straight. But she couldn't. Her bike veered into the air, into emptiness.

He didn't see her fall. She simply disappeared from the bridge—she and her bike. Abruptly he did something he had thought was impossible—he put on the brakes and jumped off onto the planks. He looked down. The water was way, way down, glistening with a dull, firm shine like a metal streaming away, somewhere beyond the bridge. He saw her bike, caught by its frame at the end of a beam, sticking out from behind the rough scaffolding, still swinging slightly. But the girl was nowhere in sight.

Stunned, Kostya put down his bike and dived.

He pierced the surface of the water with his hands

and felt it close above him as he was dragged down by the current. Although stung by the fall, he had the presence of mind to open his eyes and look for her. All he could see were hazy outlines of some huge blocks and posts. After touching the bottom, he felt himself pulled up. He turned over under the water and surfaced.

The current pulled him to the bridge span. He came close to a concrete abutment not cleared yet of some wooden casing and piles of lumber. Above, fragments of the cloudy sky seemed to be peeking through the many-storied net of girders, crossbeams and timbering. The current was strong, too strong for any resistance. Kostya drifted with it, turning, whirling, not even trying to fight it until . . . he saw her, just around the bend.

The top of her head appeared behind a pile of timber sticking out of the water at the bridge span. Up to her mouth in water, the girl clutched the pile with both hands, right in front of a foaming whirl. Kostya couldn't see her whole face but her cheek and one eye, and from the look of that eye—large, frightened—he knew that she was holding with her last strength. One more moment and the current would carry her away.

"Hold on!" he shouted, choking on a mouthful of water. Now there was only one thing to be afraid of, that the current would carry him by her. He'd never be able to get back to her against it. Kostya tried desperately to gain control of his movements. His wet breeches and canvas slippers hampered his effort. Nonetheless, he managed to throw out his left arm and grab that same pile. As the current whirled him around and around he hung on, his shoulder touching hers.

The girl's pale, wet face was close to his, her wide-open eyes bright with tension. He hoped she would believe that he would be able to save her. But how? He didn't have the slightest idea himself what to do next.

High up, the concrete abutment towered like a tremendous giant. Its surface was too smooth to offer a hold. Kostya looked back—behind them the river grew wide.

"You know how to swim?" he asked.

She shook her head.

Kostya knew that the girl couldn't hold on much longer. He looked back again; the left bank was not too far away. By himself he'd probably make it. To the right, in the direction of the current, the river made a bend. To the left, oblong stones jutted out of the water. There, he should try to get over there. . . .

He looked at the girl again. He'd have to act fast, as long as she still had some strength left. "Let go," he ordered.

"No, no."

"You must listen to me," he said gravely. He pulled her hand away from the pile and tried to put it on his shoulder. Immediately her other hand slipped off the pile and now the girl clung to him with both hands. Under the burden Kostya let go, and both of them began to sink. The whirl pulled them under. In desperation he forcibly pried open her hands and pushed her away. Thrashing wildly, the girl rose to the surface by herself. He, too, came up, snorted and looked around. The girl kept thrashing right beside him. Her round face rose for a moment out of the water; her mouth gasped for air before she began to sink again. The bridge with all its mass of iron and wood seemed to be rapidly backing away.

Kostya wound her short, chubby arm around his neck. Her other arm which was about to clutch him he pushed aside. "Don't you dare," he said sternly. "You must obey me."

She obeyed and stopped clinging to him. As they

began to float more steadily, Kostya struggled stubbornly, stroking with one arm and cutting across the current toward the stones. The girl's soft arm rested confidently though heavily against his neck, pressing his face into the water. But Kostya knew how to handle himself. As long as her face remained above water, he'd be able to lift his head for a breath of air, then let it be submerged.

The girl stopped struggling. She calmed down and obviously had more confidence in him than he had in himself. "I'll do whatever you say," she whispered into his ear. But he felt he was weakening and he was afraid the current would not let them reach the stones. He tried to drift to the shore but the whirls carried him to the right, around the stones, toward the rapids. Two times he tried to reach bottom with his feet; on the third try he touched it.

Although the water reached above his ears, he managed to keep afloat. The shallow from which the stones protruded had apparently extended quite far. Seeing him stand, the girl tried to stand up too. After she swallowed some water and choked, Kostya picked her up and, stepping carefully, he carried her to the shore.

Fifteen minutes later they were sitting on the sloping bank amid elm trees, watching the water through the branches. Their clothes were hung on the trees to dry—he had only his trunks on, she had on panties and a white undershirt. Her semi-nakedness embarrassed him; he tried not to sit too close to her, nor glance at her too often. She, however, seemed not to mind. Her innocent, bright eyes were full of confidence as they admired him through strands of wet hair that kept falling onto her face.

Their bicycles lay side by side on the grass. Kostya

had removed them from the bridge by himself. The zeal of achievement had made him feel light and fearless. It hadn't been too difficult to get his bicycle, although when he had stepped onto those planks once again he had asked himself how he was able to ride on that narrow, unfenced path. An hour ago he'd probably not have had the courage to walk on it; but now he ambled without fear, without having to look at his feet. To recover the girl's bike wasn't that easy; he had to clamber down the timbering and hoist the thing with his feet while hanging on the girder with his hands. He had enjoyed his work, however, knowing that she stood there on the shore, watching him, admiring him. He hadn't been afraid to fall into the water because that would have only been a repeat jump. But he had been concerned he might drop the bicycle. He hadn't. He rolled them both up onto the shore, toward the elm tree where their clothes were hung to dry.

"You can do everything," the girl looked at Kostya with admiring eyes.

"I can," he confirmed. "Had I dropped your bike I'd have given you mine." He felt like being extremely generous; as a matter of fact he was sorry he couldn't give her his bike.

"I'd not have taken it for anything," she said. "You are leaving?"

"Yes, tonight."

"For long?"

"Forever."

"And when will you come back?" she asked.

"Probably never."

The impression his words made on her affected him too.

"Never," the girl repeated slowly. "How far are you going?"

"Very far," he replied. "I'm taking the Moscow train tonight."

She asked if he was going to the district capital. She had apparently thought the district capital was very far.

"Uh uh," Kostya said. "The day after tomorrow I'll be in Moscow."

"In Moscow?" she asked respectfully.

"But only for a day," he explained. "Got to do some sightseeing."

"You're going even farther?" she asked incredulously.

He nodded. "To Siberia."

She became quiet. He sensed how impressive that name sounded to her.

"Who's going with you?" she asked again.

"I'm going by myself."

While he answered her questions, Kostya began to see his trip in a new light. He had suddenly made a discovery—he found out something about himself he had never known: he could accomplish tasks. The future, which up to now had appeared fearful, suddenly became a grandiose adventure within reach.

"I'll guide big ships," Kostya said, getting up from excitement. "Diesel motor ships."

"Where to?"

"To the Arctic Ocean. Beyond the Arctic Circle and back. Through the taiga, tundra, all kinds of animals," Kostya recalled what he knew about Siberia. He was waiting for her to ask if he really knew how to guide Diesel motor ships, but she didn't. Perhaps she had some doubts if he really could do everything. He, too, had some doubts.

"I'll learn," he said, thinking of Uncle Vasya. "What one man can do, another man can too."

There was silence for a while. Narrow-shouldered, long-legged, upright, Kostya stared into the water glistening through the trees. Absorbed in his new ideas, he seemed to have forgotten about the girl who sat with her arms around her knees, glancing at him timidly from time to time.

"Is somebody coming to see you off?" she asked softly.

"They are," he nodded.

"Who?"

Kostya knew that Gramma and Aunt Nadya would come with him to the station, but somehow he didn't feel like telling it to the girl. He made no reply.

"I'll come too. May I?" she asked in a pattering whisper, brushing off her wet hair from her forehead. "We live next to the station; I'll just jump out of the window and run up. May I?" the girl talked fast, as if she were afraid he might stop her. "I won't be in anybody's way; they won't even see me. I'll just watch. May I? May I?"

Kostya didn't answer. He looked at her with a joyous wonderment in his heart—it was a hitherto unknown tenderness which he realized was also a new discovery.

We Wear the Mask

We wear the mask that grins and lies,
It hides our cheeks and shades our eyes,—
This debt we pay to human guile;
With torn and bleeding hearts we smile,
And mouth with myriad subtleties.

Why should the world be overwise,
In counting all our tears and sighs?
Nay, let them only see us, while
  We wear the mask.

We smile, but, O great Christ, our cries
To Thee from tortured souls arise.
We sing, but oh, the clay is vile
Beneath our feet, and long the mile;
But let the world dream otherwise,
  We wear the mask.

Paul Laurence Dunbar

What do you think is the "mask" the speaker refers to?

Why do they continue to wear it?

Do you keep any masks handy? If so, why?

Nathan and David

(2 Samuel 11:26-27; 12:1-23)

26 When Uriah's wife heard that her husband was dead,
27 she mourned for him; and when the period of mourning
was over, David sent for her and brought her into his
house. She became his wife and bore him a son. But
what David had done was wrong in the eyes of the LORD.

1 The LORD sent Nathan the prophet to David, and
when he entered his presence, he said to him, 'There
were once two men in the same city, one rich and the
2,3 other poor. The rich man had large flocks and herds, but
the poor man had nothing of his own except one little
ewe lamb. He reared it himself, and it grew up in his
home with his own sons. It ate from his dish, drank
from his cup and nestled in his arms; it was like a
4 daughter to him. One day a traveller came to the rich
man's house, and he, too mean to take something from
his own flocks and herds to serve to his guest, took the
5 poor man's lamb and served up that.' David was very
angry, and burst out, 'As the LORD lives, the man who
6 did this deserves to die! He shall pay for the lamb four
times over, because he has done this and shown no pity.'
7 Then Nathan said to David, 'You are the man. This is
the word of the LORD the God of Israel to you: "I
anointed you king over Israel, I rescued you from the
8 power of Saul, I gave you your master's daughter and
his wives to be your own, I gave you the daughters of
Israel and Judah; and, had this not been enough, I
9 would have added other favours as great. Why then have
you flouted the word of the LORD by doing what is
wrong in my eyes? You have struck down Uriah the
Hittite with the sword; the man himself you murdered
by the sword of the Ammonites, and you have stolen his
10 wife. Now, therefore, since you have despised me and
taken the wife of Uriah the Hittite to be your own wife,
your family shall never again have rest from the sword."
This is the word of the LORD: "I will bring trouble
11 upon you from within your own family; I will take your
wives and give them to another man before your eyes,
and he will lie with them in broad daylight. What you
12 did was done in secret; but I will do this in the light of
the day for all Israel to see." ' David said to Nathan, 'I

have sinned against the LORD.' Nathan answered him, 13
'The LORD has laid on another the consequences of
your sin: you shall not die, but, because in this you have
shown your contempt for the LORD, the boy that will 14
be born to you shall die.'

When Nathan had gone home, the LORD struck the 15
boy whom Uriah's wife had borne to David, and he was
very ill. David prayed to God for the child; he fasted 16
and went in and spent the night fasting, lying on the
ground. The older men of his household tried to get him 17
to rise from the ground, but he refused and would eat
no food with them. On the seventh day the boy died, 18
and David's servants were afraid to tell him. 'While the
boy was alive,' they said, 'we spoke to him, and he did
not listen to us; how can we now tell him that the boy is
dead? He may do something desperate.' But David saw 19
his servants whispering among themselves and guessed
that the boy was dead. He asked, 'Is the boy dead?', and
they answered, 'He is dead.' Then David rose from the 20
ground, washed and anointed himself, and put on fresh
clothes; he entered the house of the LORD and pros-
trated himself there. Then he went home, asked for food
to be brought, and when it was ready, he ate it. His ser- 21
vants asked him, 'What is this? While the boy lived you
fasted and wept for him, but now that he is dead you rise
up and eat.' He answered, 'While the boy was still alive I 22
fasted and wept, thinking, "It may be that the LORD
will be gracious to me, and the boy may live." But now 23
that he is dead, why should I fast? Can I bring him back
again? I shall go to him; he will not come back to me.'

The New English Bible

"You know what you must do," he said.

"Yes," I said, "I'll go and tell him before he finds out himself."

"D-Day"

Bush Boy, Poor Boy

James Aldridge

Once, there were two things that were worthwhile doing in life. One was to shoot a fox. The other was to catch a twenty-pound cod. At one time these things were very important to me. I gave up everything in life to them. Why, I couldn't exactly say. But the reason began somewhere in the difference between myself—a bush boy and a poor boy—and young Tom Woodley, who was a town boy and a rich boy.

I lived with my father. He was a woodcutter. We lived near the Murray River, three or four miles outside the town of St. Helen, Victoria. The truth is, I didn't know much about anything except the bush. But young Tom Woodley was a clever boy with everything he touched: school, sports, church-going. He was liked by everybody in the town. That included the teachers and the policemen. Where Tom was the best of everything, I was the worst of it, except in the bush. Every boy in town had something he could laugh at me about. But once they came out of the town and along the river, I could beat them all. That was until young Tom Woodley came out to the river in his father's Model-T Ford on a picnic. Within an hour he had shot a fox with a .22 rifle. He had also pulled in a fifteen-pound Murray-cod on a line.

These were things that I, a bush boy, had never done. I had caught a lot of fish. I had even caught a Murray-cod of ten pounds. But never anything larger. When I could get ammunition, I had shot large numbers of rabbits. In fact I almost lived by selling rabbit skins. But I had never once been able to get a fox in range.

With Tom Woodley I knew it had been luck. But that

didn't do me any good because I knew that I had nothing to stand up to now, nothing at all. I stopped going into the town altogether. In fact I even stopped going to school. I stayed in the bush, wanting to catch a twenty-pound cod and shoot a fox before facing the laughter of the boys in shoes and the joking of men behind counters.

The fox would be hard to kill. Yet the day came when I was to stand near enough to a fox to club it to death, if only I had been big enough to do it.

It was really an accident. For once, I was not hunting or fishing, but looking for mushrooms. I was on Pental Island, which was covered with lagoons and swamps and dry patches and clumps. As I was walking through a shallow fish pool, I came out on a small dry rise with one clumpy bush on it. I was picking mushrooms under the bush when I saw the fox. He had smelled me, but there was nowhere for him to go. He was more afraid of the water than he was of me. He backed away from the bush. I backed away from him. The dry land we shared was only about thirty feet square. He was less than ten yards away. But here I was without a gun. There was the fox, standing with his tail up and his teeth bared, but not making a sound.

I stepped slowly back into the water. I couldn't do anything without a gun. I knew it would take me an hour to get home: I had to swim a river and then go over a mile through the bush. Even so, I knew that this fox would stay right where he was. I knew foxes. I knew that this one was terrified of the water and would die before he would move into it. So I put down the mushrooms I had collected in a sugar bag and got through the pool and started to run for home.

At home I had a .22 rifle. But the very reason I didn't have it with me was that I didn't have ammunition. As I ran I begged myself to think of a place where I could find just one shell: no more. I thought of the .22 shell I had lost last year in the woodpile. That was no good. I had tried a dozen times before to find it. I could not borrow any. There weren't any shells in all the drawers in the house. I had looked for them time and time before. I was running for nothing, but I didn't stop. I ran through the high grass and came to the river. I jumped off the point and swam across the deep hole and waded the rest. Then I ran up the high bank, through the willow trees, and made for home.

I got home and started to hunt in the woodpile, raking up the chips with my hands and feet, still panting and puffing from the run. I couldn't find that .22 in the dust and the chips of a year ago. I went desperately into the house. I looked in the chamber of my rifle. But it was empty. I had known, but I had hoped. Then I knew there was only one thing to do. My father was away cutting wood, so I went into his room and got the .303 that hung on the wall. It was so big that I could hardly carry it. But I lifted it down. It had a clip of three shells in the magazine. It was clean, but it hadn't been fired for years. My father wouldn't even fire it himself. The shells were in it in case of emergency. I took it down and carried it outside. This was the worst thing I could do. I was not allowed to touch this gun, not to touch it at all. But I didn't care now.

I put the heavy .303 over my shoulder like a log, and started to run back with it. I was tired already, and I was half-walking before I had gone far. Still, I kept running in spasms, I walked and ran, and when I got to the river I nearly sank trying to keep the gun out of water. I couldn't hold it up, and it was well dipped by the time I got across.

I covered the distance from the river to the lagoon very slowly. I was starting to shake inside, puffing in and out. But I was able to run the last hundred yards to the swamp and the pool. I looked across the twenty-five yards of water to the island. At the same time I pulled back the bolt of the .303 and put a shell in the chamber. Then I waded across to kill my fox.

But the fox had gone. I kicked the bush and looked into it, looking for a hole. But there was nothing at all, except a few droppings and a feather. He had gone and that was that. I couldn't see how he could get off, knowing his terror of water. I started to hunt on the other dry patches, and then on the whole dry land. It was hopeless. So I went home with my mushrooms and the .303.

I got a hiding with a harness strap for taking the .303, because I couldn't give any explanation of why I had taken it. I did not try to tell the truth. I simply made up a long story about chasing a wild pig. My father said there were no wild pigs in the whole country. I knew that too, but I got the hiding anyway.

I went back looking for that fox the next day and thereafter. I kept looking and hunting, even though I had no ammunition. Then one night I cried for a couple of hours in bed. The next day I went back to fishing for a twenty-pound cod.

There were a number of places along the Little Murray River which were good for cod. I knew them all. The best was at Old Roy Carmichael's. Roy had a house which he had built out of a boiler. Outside (near the river) there was a gate he had taken from some old church. But there wasn't any fence. On the gate there was a latch that said IN and OUT. Roy always put it on the right one if he was in or out. He had built mud steps down to the water's edge. As the river rose in winter and went down in summer, Roy would mark the height on the steps with an iron peg. I used this peg to hold my rod as I fished for cod. Old Roy himself came down to get some water just as I was putting bait on a hook.

"Why don't you use worms?" he asked me.

"I've used up just about every worm in the countryside," I told him.

Roy was thin and old. He had a gray mustache that dropped right over his mouth. Sometimes he laughed for no reason at all, and he laughed now.

"How is your father, Edgar?" he asked me.

"He went into town to sell some wood," I told him.

"How do you like it when they laugh at him in town?" Roy said.

I didn't know what to say to that. So I asked him why he lived in the boiler.

"I lived over it for twenty years," he said. "Now I live in it. That's the best boiler that ever went into a riverboat. They don't make them like it anymore. If she hadn't hit the Point, the old Rang Dang would be going yet, with that boiler still inside her."

I knew all about it. The old Rang Dang was a paddle steamer which had tried to come up the Little Murray. It had hit low ground at the Point and sunk. Old Roy had been the captain of it. He had waited around to try and get the Rang Dang up from the bottom. But the boat had fallen apart. So he had only saved the boiler. He had stayed right there and lived in the boiler. That was a long time ago. I had asked him once why he didn't get another boat. He had picked up a dead sunflower and thrown it at me. So I hadn't asked him again. My father, Edgar Allan, had told me that he couldn't get another boat anywhere after that. They, I suppose whoever owned the boat, said he was drunk when he hit the

Point. After that Roy never drank, just to prove that he had not been drunk at the time.

"What are you fishing for?" he asked me.

"A big cod," I told him. "Twenty-pounder." And I told Roy about Tom Woodley and the fox and the cod.

"Have you been getting any cod lately?" I asked.

"No. Perch. That's all there is in this river. Yellow bellies."

"Fish are fish," I said.

"Why don't you go over to the Big Murray?"

"The river is still too high to swim."

"I'll take you over in the boat."

"No, thanks," I said very quickly. Roy had taken me over once before, saying he would pick me up when I came back, if I shouted to him. I had come back and shouted. He hadn't come. He had forgotten all about me. The river had been too high to swim, so I had stayed on Pental Island all night, getting a hiding when I went home the next day.

"I'll come over with you," he said. "I'm getting sick of the taste of perch."

"All right," I said.

Roy went to get some lines and the oars to his boat. His boat was always tied up here at the steps. He had built it himself. It was the best small-boat on the river.

Roy came down and looked at my rod and said: "What do you want a rod for? A line is better for cod. They are like elephants: they catch themselves."

"I like a rod," I said. I liked to fish with a rod. If I caught that twenty-pounder I wanted to catch it on a rod.

"Leave it behind," Roy said.

"It's all right. I want to take it."

Roy shouted. "Whatever-your-name-is, leave that rod behind!"

I stood there and didn't get into the boat.

"Are you coming or aren't you?" Roy shouted. He was red in the face.

"If I can bring the rod."

"Get in," he said. "Get in. Bring the rod. What do I care? You're like the rest of them. You can laugh at me! Get in. Do you hear me!"

He was shouting at the top of his voice. He shouted and swore all the way over. As we went across we were carried downstream by the current. But Roy knew just where it would take him. He had another set of steps on the Pental Island side of the river, and we landed right on them.

At the timber we walked straight through to the deep hole under a tree.

"You can take the dead tree," Roy said. This was the best place. I thanked him. But it did not mean anything because wherever I fished, he would cast his line near mine and then come around by me and talk. He didn't believe that noise scared off the fish.

Now I walked out on the dead tree and sat on a fork. Half of the dead tree was in the water. I could drop the line straight down into the hole; but I like to cast a bit. I baited the hook. Then I let about a yard of line hang on the end of the rod, put my thumb on the wooden reel, and swung the rod. The sinker flew out, taking the line; and it plunked down right where I wanted it. Roy undid a heavy cord line from a stick and baited it. Then he swung it over his head and threw it. The bolt which acted as a sinker plunked down very near mine; too near. I jumped, because I believe noise frightens fish.

We sat quietly for a while, and I held the line lightly, waiting for bites. Then Roy got up and walked over to the tree and came out on it.

"Why don't you go to school?" he said to me.

"It is too far away," I said.

"School is never too far away," he said. "You could walk."

"It takes too long," I said. "Two hours."

"What are two hours! Can you read and write?"

"Yes," I said. I could read very little. I could hardly write. Most people thought I would say "No," when they asked me that. But I didn't like saying "No."

"That's not enough," Roy Carmichael said. "You have to know about figures and some history."

"I know," I said. "I would like to know about them."

"Yes. You ought to go to Castle Donnington School."

"I used to go," I told him, "but Miss Gillespie sent me home."

"What for?" Roy was angry straightaway.

"She said I was pretty dirty. I didn't have any books. It wasn't any good having them. I used to swim the river to save time, and I accidentally dropped the books in the river near the Point one day. They were no good when I got them up. It's funny she thought I was dirty. I had to swim the river every day."

"What does it matter if you're dirty? What's the matter with dirt?"

I was getting small bites, nibbles. I could imagine the fish just pulling on the side of the bait, tearing it away without touching the hook. So I waited. Then it all happened.

"Look at your line," I said to Roy.

He looked over to the bank, and the willow springer to which he had tied his line had been pulled clean out of the bank, and was tight in the water. Before he could leave me, I felt a big pull—a tremendous pull—on my own rod, and I jerked it up to hook the fish; but the rod bent and nearly broke, and I knew I had my big one.

"You've hooked my line," Roy shouted in my ear. "You'll lose my fish."

"It's on mine," I cried back, as I held onto the rod, almost falling into the water, just hanging on.

"No," Roy said. "You've hooked my line. Give me the rod."

He was dancing up and down. His face was red, and his hair was flying. "You'll lose my line, you're pulling it in. You'll lose the fish."

I didn't have time to look around at Roy's line. I was trying to hang onto the fish that had hold of mine, and at the same time keep Roy from taking my rod away from me.

"What's the matter with you!" Roy said and got a good grip on my rod. "Let it go or I'll break it on your back."

The fish pulled, the rod bent, Roy and I held onto it.

Then Roy swung his arm and knocked me clean off the log into the shallow water behind, and by the time I got out he was reeling in the fish and walking back to the bank to land it. I ran over and tried to get the rod back, but he pushed me away and landed the fish.

It was a Murray-cod all right, and it was more than twenty pounds. It was fat and gasping and kicking as Roy shipped it right up the bank away from the water. I ran up to get hold of the line. I could see already who had caught it.

"It was on my hook, it was on my line," I cried at Roy, and I was really crying. "You caught my fish." It had been Roy's line that had tangled with mine: it was his that had ruined this catch. "You caught my fish," was all I could shout at him.

"What's the matter with you?" Roy said. I thought he was going to hit me again. "I got the fish out, didn't

I? You would have let it go. You would have fallen in the hole. You would have lost it."

"You got my fish," I said. "That's the fish I've been waiting to catch."

"Well, you caught it," Roy said. He put his foot on the cod to take out the hook.

"I didn't catch it," I said. "You did!"

"It was on your line," he said. He was laughing now.

"What's the good of that! You pulled it in. You caught it. You took my fish away from me. You caught my fish!"

"Well, you can have it," Roy said.

"I don't want it. I just wanted to catch it."

"Well, you caught it. You can say you caught it. I won't deny it."

"That's no good," I cried. "Tom Woodley caught his fifteen-pounder. You should have let me catch this one." I was not exactly howling. But I was practically screaming at Roy, because I knew that I would have little or no chance of ever again catching another big one.

Roy was sorry and said: "Never mind, Edgar."

I swore then, round and long.

Roy got mad again and threw a clod at me.

"You stole my fish," I said from a distance, to insult.

"Take your fish!" he shouted.

"I don't want it," I said, and then I ran.

I tried to get Roy's boat out and back across the river, but I beached it on some shallows, and Roy caught me and took it over and laughed at me all the way across. Then he held onto me, on the other side. I said I'd never get a fish like that and never get a fox. Never again. I was finished now. Roy knew it. He hung onto me and told me he would let the world know I had caught that fish. And he would help me get that fox. He had ammunition and a fox whistle. If I came back tomorrow he would hunt a fox and maybe fish again. Then he let me go.

"Don't you want your rod?" he called after me as I went.

"Keep it," I shouted back and swore at him again.

He threw it at me. I ran away cursing and shouting, leaving my rod, and leaving the big Murray-cod that should have been mine.

That cod was mine, and I knew it. Yet not having it, and not having caught it, the thing began to overwhelm me. It was always on my mind, from the time I lost it. Before long it had become something that I had but could never have: something I had done yet could never do. The puzzle and mystery of this was even worse than the mystery of the disappearing fox. This gave me the same feeling: to have wanted something so much, to have almost had it, and then to have lost it at the moment of success. It made me sick. I was never in peace again. I had to kill that fox to solve these things, to give me back a day without thought and a night without terror. I knew I had to do it or I would be unhappy forever.

Then late in summer Roy gave me my chance. He found me one day on Pental Island. After he had boxed my ears for taking a revenge shot at his dog, he began to laugh at me.

"Are you still bawling and howling about that fish?" he said to me.

I hadn't forgiven him even then for that fish. He had certainly told the town I had caught it (a twenty-eight-pounder). He had thus half-saved me from Tom Woodley and the town boys. But I hadn't forgiven him because I knew I hadn't caught it. I wouldn't talk to him about the fish. But he laughed and didn't care. So I didn't care. I told him I would call the next day and get my rod back.

"Do you still want that fox, Edgar?" he asked me.

"Yes, but I want to get it myself," I told him.

"Don't be such a baby," he said. "And if you do want a fox, you come down here tomorrow morning before daybreak and I'll show you where you can get one."

"Where is he?" I asked Roy. I didn't trust him now.

"You come down tomorrow morning and I'll show you," he shouted.

"You'll show me where it is, and then you'll shoot it yourself," I said.

"You holy little beggar boy," he called me with a red face. He seemed very upset. I was sorry. "You come down here tomorrow morning before light and I'll take you over and get you that fox! D'you hear!"

"All right," I said.

I don't think I slept at all that night. I knew that Roy would really show me a fox, within shooting range. By now, hunting the fox had become habit. I just didn't know where I stood these days. More and more all things had become a puzzle to me because of the loss of that fish. Yet on this night I knew it would end. Tomorrow I would hunt that fox, shoot it, finish this whole thing, and go back to normal again. That was tomorrow.

I was over at Roy's long before light. I had to kick on the boiler door to wake him up. He told me to go away and leave him in peace. But I kept on kicking the door and he finally got up. He gave me a piece of cold meat to eat. We rowed across to Pental Island. Roy knew Pental Island even better than I did, because he had a trap line all over it. He covered it almost every day. We emptied a few of his traps as we went. He had me carrying the rabbits on my shoulder as he walked ahead.

"Don't make so much noise," he said to me, as we climbed a little hill. The rabbits were hitting my back, and their bellies were making a rolling and rumbling sound. "Drop those things and keep quiet," he said in a whisper.

Roy didn't creep, as I would in hunting. He walked upright. But he walked very carefully and slowly, stopping still from time to time and then moving on again. I moved behind him, doing what he did, and holding my .22 loaded and ready. When we reached the dry, red top of the hill, which was bare and round, Roy lay down carefully and put his head over the top. It was still dark, but light was breaking the sky.

"Down there," Roy whispered, "that old fox is sleeping there now."

"I can't see him," I said.

"Of course you can't," Roy growled between his teeth. "He'll be coming out when the sun comes up. Can you hit him from here?"

It was about fifty feet down to the clump, and if the fox wasn't running I knew I could hit him. "Leave him to me," I said because I didn't want Roy to get in my way. He had a .22 himself. He held it ready for use.

We waited. I had a feeling now that this was all right. It was simple enough to be lying here. It was simple enough for anything in life at all. The sun would rise. The fox would come out. I would shoot, and life would again be normal. I had never felt so sure in my whole life before. I looked at Roy and cocked a grin. I was forgiving him the cod.

"Keep your eye on that bush," Roy whispered angrily.

I watched the bush and watched the horizon. The sky

became pink, the birds flew high. And then came the sun; and a little after the sun came the fox.

He was old and red. He had white feet, a white tip on his tail, and alert ears. He came out of a hole near the bush. He put his head around quickly and lifted his nose up and crouched. Then he walked a few feet as if the ground was hot right under him. He turned around and looked straight up at the hill. Then he sat on his tail and licked his paw. I had my rifle to my face.

My .22 was old and the sight was off. So I sighted below and to the left of his head. It was easy and sure. The chance was here, the world was sure. Just as he licked the side of his jaws, I was easing on the trigger.

Yet I didn't fire. Whatever the reason, I didn't want to kill that fox and I didn't plan to. I held the sight and kept my cheek on the gun and the finger on the trigger. I thought to myself that all I must do is give it a pull and that fox would be dead, and I would be alive.

"Go on," Roy said as if he would kill me himself for being a fool.

"I don't want him," I said and put down the gun.

"Shoot!" he said right in my ear.

"I don't want him!" I said aloud and the fox heard and was gone like a shot. Roy stood up and I could see his .22 follow the fox for the first few seconds. Then he fired. I was still lying down, but I saw the old red fox go tumbling over. But I didn't care. At the same moment another one came leaping out of the warren and went running away, full of life.

"Why didn't you shoot!" Roy cried as he reloaded his gun.

"I don't know," I said. I really didn't know.

"Are you sick or something?"

I shook my head. I thought for a moment that I would like to stay on this hill forever.

Roy looked hard at me and laughed for no reason and forgot about the fox. He sat down on the warm side of the hill.

"How old are you, boy?" he asked.

"Fourteen now," I told him, still waiting for his temper.

"Fourteen," he said slowly. "Do you know how old I was when I lost the Rang Dang, lost my boat, lost everything, and never got it back?"

I didn't know and I didn't care.

"Fifty-two," he said. "Fifty-two."

I had no idea what he was talking about. He had lost something and never got it back. For my part I only knew that I was quietly happy again without knowing why.

If I had hoped to solve the problem of life by killing a fox for the loss of the cod, I knew I was wrong. Life was life, somehow. That fox had been too alive for me to shoot. The fish didn't matter. The fox didn't matter. Tom Woodley and the town boys didn't matter. And though I had spared one life to learn so much, I had killed five or six rabbits by the time we went home.

Yes, life was life; but I had it licked.

Why do you think the boy didn't shoot?

He killed rabbits on the way home, but not the fox. Why? Did he want to prove something to Roy?

How do you explain the last line?

The Brave Man of Golo

Hausa Traditional

retold by Harold Courlander

A man named Seidu lived in the village of Golo. Whenever the men of his village went hunting and returned with game, Seidu said to his wife, "Among all the hunters, I was the bravest. Single-handed I fought with the leopard and chased the elephant. I went forward with my spear, and the lion fled. I am the bravest of hunters."

His wife, Ladi, replied, "Did no one but you bring back meat?"

Seidu said, "Yes, because of my fearlessness, the others also had good luck."

Again, when it was said that the enemy was approaching, Seidu went into the bush country with the men, and when he returned, he hung his spear on the wall and said to his wife, "The enemy came forward; I went forward. When I ran at them, they turned and fled. My reputation has spread everywhere. I am the bravest of warriors. What is your opinion?"

Ladi answered, "It is so."

There was a funeral one time in another village, and some of the women of Golo wished to go. But the men were working in the fields and could not leave their work. Ladi told the women, "My husband is the bravest of men. He will take us through the forest."

She went to Seidu, saying, "The women who are going to the funeral agree that you are the one to take them through the forest. Will you go?"

Seidu said, "From one day to another no one mentions my courage. But when courage is needed, people ask, 'Where is Seidu?' Nevertheless, I will come."

He took his spear and went with the women through the forest.

There were warriors of the enemy in the forest. They were hunting game. When they saw Seidu coming with the women, they said, "Look how the man struts like a guinea cock. Let us strike fear into him."

They waited near the trail, and when the people of Golo came, the hunters came out of the brush before them and behind them.

Seidu shouted, "We are surrounded! Run for the trees!"

The women ran among the trees. Seidu ran with them. But there were enemy among the trees, and they seized all the people from Golo.

The leader of the hunters said to Seidu's wife, "What is your name?"

She replied, "Ladi."

He said, "Ladi is a name used by the women of our tribe also. Because you are called Ladi, we shall not hurt you."

He said to another woman, "What is your name?"

Seeing how good it was to be named Ladi, the woman replied, "My name too is Ladi."

The leader of the hunters said, "A good name; we shall not hurt you."

He asked another woman, and she too replied, "Ladi." All of the women were asked, and all of them answered, "My name is Ladi."

Then the leader of the hunters spoke to Seidu. "All the women of your village are named Ladi. It is a strange custom. In our village each woman has a different name. But you, guinea cock who leads the guinea hens, what are you called?"

"I," Seidu said, "I too am called Ladi. My name is Ladi also."

When the hunters heard Seidu's reply, they laughed. The leader of the hunters declared, "No, it is not possible. Ladi is a woman's name. You are a man with a spear. Do not tell me that the men of your village are also called Ladi?"

Seidu said, "No, no, only the women are called Ladi."

The hunters said, "How then are you called Ladi?"

Seidu looked one way and another way, but he saw no chance of escape. He said, "You see, appearances are deceiving. I also am a woman."

The enemy laughed. They could not stop laughing. The women of Golo laughed too.

Seidu's wife spoke. She said, "He speaks badly of himself. He is the courageous Seidu, the famous Seidu."

Seidu said then, "Yes, it is so."

A hunter said, "People say that Seidu claims to be the bravest of all men."

"No," Seidu replied, "it is no longer so. *Formerly* I was the bravest of all men. Today it is different. From now on I shall be only the bravest in my village."

The hunters let them go. Seidu and the women went to the funeral, and they returned afterward to their own houses. When they arrived in Golo, everyone was laughing at Seidu. Instead of calling him by his name, they called him Ladi. He went into his house and closed the door. Whenever he came out, they laughed. He could not hide from the shame.

At last he sent his wife to tell them this, "Seidu who was formerly the bravest of men was reduced to being the bravest in his village. But from now on he is not the bravest in the village. He agrees to be only as brave as other people."

So the people of Golo stopped ridiculing Seidu. And thereafter he was no braver than anyone else.

Fable for When There's No Way Out

Grown too big for his skin,
and it grown hard,

without a sea and atmosphere—
he's drunk it all up—

his strength's inside him now,
but there's no room to stretch.

He pecks at the top
but his beak's too soft;

though instinct and ambition shoves,
he can't get through.

Barely old enough to bleed
and already bruised!

In a case this tough
what's the use

if you break your head
instead of the lid?

Despair tempts him
to just go limp:

Maybe the cell's
already a tomb,

and beginning end
in this round room.

Still, stupidly he pecks
and pecks, as if from under

his own skull—
yet makes no crack . . .

No crack until
he finally cracks,

and kicks and stomps.
What a thrill

and shock to feel
his little gaff poke

through the floor!
A way he hadn't known or meant.

Rage works if reason won't.
When locked up, bear down.

May Swenson

Has your life borne out the statement in the last stanza? How? Are there other alternatives "when there's no way out"?

Sonnet 73

That time of year thou mayst in me behold
When yellow leaves, or none, or few, do hang
Upon those boughs which shake against the cold,
Bare ruined choirs, where late the sweet birds sang.
In me thou see'st the twilight of such day
As after sunset fadeth in the west;
Which by and by black night doth take away,
Death's second self that seals up all in rest.
In me thou see'st the glowing of such fire,
That on the ashes of his youth doth lie,
As the deathbed whereon it must expire,
Consumed with that which it was nourished by.
This thou perceiv'st, which makes thy love more strong,
To love that well which thou must leave ere long.

William Shakespeare

What do the images in the poem tell you about the speaker's age and point of view?

Do you share his perception about love?

The Father

Björnstjerne Björnson

The man about whom this story is told was the mightiest in his parish. His name was Thord Overaas. He stood one day in the pastor's study, tall and serious.

"I have been given a son," he said, "and wish to have him christened."

"What shall he be called?"

"Finn, after my father."

"And the sponsors?"

They were named, and were the best men and women in the community of the father's family.

"Is there anything further?" asked the minister, looking up.

The peasant hesitated a little. "I prefer to have him christened alone," he said.

"That is, on a week day?"

"On next Saturday, twelve, noon."

"Is there anything further?" asked the pastor.

"There is nothing further."

The peasant fumbled his cap, as if he were about to go. Then the pastor rose.

"This much further," he said, and walked over to Thord, took his hand and looked him in the eyes. "God grant that the child may be a blessing to you."

Sixteen years after that day Thord stood again in the pastor's study.

"You carry your years well, Thord," said the minister, seeing no change in him.

"Neither have I any cares," answered Thord.

To this the pastor remained silent, but after a while he asked:

"What is your errand this evening?"

"This evening I come to see about my son, who is to be confirmed tomorrow."

"He is a bright boy."

"I did not wish to pay the pastor before I knew what number he is to have on the floor."

"He shall stand number one."

"So I heard—and here is ten dollars for the pastor."

"Is there anything further?" asked the minister, looking up at Thord.

"There is nothing further." Thord went away.

Again eight years passed, then a noise was heard one day outside the pastor's study, for many men came and Thord first. The pastor looked up and recognized him.

"You come strong in numbers this evening."

"I wish to ask to have the banns pronounced for my son: he is to be married to Karen Storliden, daughter of Gudmund, who stands here."

"She is the richest girl in the parish."

"They say so," answered the peasant, smoothing back his hair with one hand.

The minister sat for a time as if in thought. He said nothing, but registered the names in his books, and the men signed accordingly.

Thord laid three dollars on the table.

"I should have only one," said the pastor.

"I know it, too, but he is my only child—I wish to do well by you."

The pastor took the money.

"It is the third time now you stand here in behalf of your son, Thord."

"But now I am through with him," said Thord. He folded his pocketbook together, and said good-by and went. The men followed slowly after.

A fortnight after that day the father and son rowed in calm weather across the water to Storliden to confer about the wedding.

"This board does not lie securely under me," said the son, and got up to lay it aright. Just then the plank on which he stood slipped; he threw out his arms, gave a cry, and fell into the water.

"Take hold of the oar!" called the father, rising and

holding it toward him. But when the son had made a few strokes he stiffened.

"Wait a little!" cried the father, and rowed nearer. Then the son turned over backward, gave a long look at the father—and sank.

Thord would not believe it. He held the boat still and stared at the spot where his son had sunk down as if he were to come up again. Some bubbles rose to the surface, then a few more, then just one large one that burst—and the sea lay again like a mirror.

For three days and three nights they saw the father rowing about that spot without food or sleep; he was searching for his son. On the third day in the morning he found him, and came carrying him over the hills to his farm.

A year perhaps had passed since that day. Then the pastor, late one autumn evening, heard something in the hallway outside his door fumbling cautiously for the latch. The minister opened the door and in stepped a tall, bent man, thin and white-haired. The minister looked long at him before he recognized him; it was Thord.

"Do you come so late?" said the pastor, and stood still before him.

"Oh, yes, I come late," said Thord, seating himself.

The pastor also sat down as if waiting. There was a long silence, then Thord said: "I have something with me that I wish to give to the poor; it shall be in the form of a legacy and carry my son's name." He got up, laid money on the table, and sat down again.

The pastor counted the money. "That is a great deal," he said.

"It is half of my farm; I sold it today."

The minister remained sitting a long time in silence;

finally he asked gently: "What are you now going to do, Thord?"

"Something better."

They sat for a time, Thord with his eyes upon the floor, and the pastor with his eyes upon Thord. Finally the pastor said slowly: "Now I believe your son has finally become a blessing to you."

"Yes, now I think so myself," said Thord.

He looked up and two tears rolled heavily down over his face.

Maybe the measure of a man is what he thinks about things. In what sense is that true of Thord?

D-Day

Cor W. Barendrecht

There was a strange sensation in the air. I had about the same feeling when German airplanes came flying so low I could see the crosses on their bellies. I saw their shadows coming down the bay window in the family room. They were shadows like the Greek crosses on the bellies of the planes, only bigger ones. There was shooting from machine guns and mortars. A shadow came down and shattered abruptly, diffusing the light on the window in a strange mixture of light and shade. An airplane exploded in the air and a burning wing barely missed the house.

"Get away from that window," dad shouted.

I didn't understand what it was all about. Everything happened as in a dizzy spell. The shadows, the explosions, the anti-aircraft fire that followed, the simultaneous howling of the sirens on the rooftops, the shouting, and the sudden sense of panic that came over me seemed like grey clouds hovering low over my head. I felt as if I was locked up between heaven and earth. I used to get the feeling while walking in the density of the forest with mountains ahead and mountains behind. And beyond and around the mountains were other mountains, as high and as threatening as the first ones.

"War," dad said. "We must all stay inside until the clear signal."

We went to the unused room, which was sheltered by four brick walls. One wall had a small high window, too high to reach. Besides, it had been pasted shut with wallpaper, so it really did not serve any purpose. There were old pieces of furniture that were never used. Sentimental value only; old family pieces and some that belonged to the folks' starter set.

We made thin strips from old newspapers and pasted them in a checkered pattern on the bay windows. The paper would keep the windows from breaking when the house was trembling because of the bombing and shooting. It might save a life if chips of hand grenades flew into the window. The paper would hold the pieces of glass together.

I had looked out into the street through these windows for four years, and nothing ever seemed different. The electric lantern in front of the house had not been lit for months because there was no power in the line. The gloomy three-story buildings were leaning together, making the entire street look like a solid wall of brick. The road between the two massive blocks of buildings was paved with cobblestones, discolored here and there with patches of manure, dropped in passing by the horse of the milkman and the horse of the bread peddler. The sidewalk of grey patio stones was offset by five lantern posts at regular intervals from one end of the street to the other. The lanterns were all identical, except for the lower parts, which were faded from the abuse of street dogs. The dogs came two or more, stopping briefly at the lantern post, lifting one leg, and moving on to the next post. The street was ugly, but I looked at it so often that I no longer noticed how unsightly it really was.

But today there was something different about the street. The Nazis who lived halfway down the block were loading their belongings onto a hand cart. They wore black uniforms with red patches on the shoulders. On the round collars the letters SS were embroidered in gold. There were also some German soldiers standing on the street corner. The one with the chrome button on his collar talked a lot with short, impatient gestures. Then they all raised their right hands and clicked their heels. I could hear the thump like a hundred steel shovels all dropped at the same time. They marched off, shouting, "Sieg Heil! Sieg Heil!" a little faster at every step.

When they turned the corner, the street was silent again. Across the street a door opened and to my surprise I saw dad hurriedly crossing the street. He seemed small against the tall buildings. He measured a lucky five foot six with his shoes on.

"Most of a man's work is close to the ground," he would say in a jesting way. He took me for long walks through the nearby woods. He liked to walk with a cane which he used to push the brush aside and to point out unusual specimens of nature. He stopped to show me a wildflower hidden under the ferns and greens, and seemed to know every plant by its common and Latin name. But he could also put down the stick and use his bare hands when a verbal correction needed reinforcement.

With short, impatient steps he walked toward our apartment.

"What did the B.B.C. say?" mother asked as she opened the door.

"The Germans are being pushed eastwards at Normandy, and the National Socialists are getting scared and are moving ahead. It can't last much longer."

"Thank God." She was holding his hands in hers.

"I must go now. Take care of the kids."

"Be careful. I'll leave the door unlocked."

"Dad working tonight?" I asked when she came back from the portal.

"Yes, a dangerous job these days," she said. There was concern in her voice. She worried when dad went out. Not only was his vision very poor at night, but he also lacked all sense of direction in the darkness. He had papers that permitted him to be on the street after curfew time, but they did not guarantee his safety. After that night when the Nazis had dropped a gasoline can from the rooftop he had become a little more careful.

She sat down near the fireplace and picked up a basketful of socks that needed mending. She selected one with a hole the size of an egg and seemed determined to devote the entire evening to the inhuman task before her. Then her skilful hand stuck the needle into the sock, a little way up from the edge, and travelled across the vacuum to the other side, again a little from the edge. Then the needle moved over a strand, and dragging a thin cotton thread behind it, moved back again. Mother kept manipulating thread and needle until a pattern became visible over the gap. I had found a warm spot on the floor near the fireplace and watched her spinning her web.

"What's dad doing outside at night?" I asked.

Mother dropped the sock in her lap and held her index finger over her mouth.

"The less that is said, the better it is," she said.

"But dad said it can't last much longer."

"That is what he said," she said slowly. She did not seem to believe as yet that the war would be over almost any time. Her eyes were staring at an empty brass candlestick standing over the fireplace as if it were a religious relic.

"I still hear the footstep of soldiers down the street. The rain hits the window and rushes down the down-spouts. They stop at our house and ring the bell and pound the windows as if there were a holocaust.

" 'Is there any copper or brass in the house?' they said in German.

" 'Nothing,' I said. It was the truth. The little copper we had was an old vase from grandma and an old-fashioned hot coal footwarmer, and these items were hidden in the toolshed behind the house.

" 'Where is your husband?' said a young soldier. He didn't look older than eighteen.

" 'I'll call him.' I brought your father from the back yard where he was tending roses—the only thing of beauty they left him.

" 'Yes?' he said.

" 'Show your papers,' said the soldier.

"Dad showed his identification papers.

" 'Your age and occupation still the same?'

" 'No and yes; what's this all about?'

" 'All men between eighteen and forty are to report to headquarters. Come with us.'

"They took him to the East school where they made

their quarters and forced him to work as a heating engineer. In a way he was lucky; the other men they took were digging manholes in frozen soil.

" 'I don't really mind the work,' your father said. But he was developing a little nervous twitch on his left eye which told the truth more accurately than his rationalizing words.

"And now he goes to heat the fires every night. And after that he does some work for the underground about which he does not talk even to me. I just hope nothing happens to him before the end is here."

It had grown dark in the family room. Mother drew the black window shades to prevent the light from shining out into the street. She looked tired. Deep grooves curved under her eyes. She lit a paraffin lamp. By the light that fell on her face I saw that she had a deep wrinkle on her forehead. Her blue eyes seemed even warmer in the light. A thin line of smoke rose to the ceiling. It made black spots on the plaster. While looking at the smoke and the curdling forms above me, the feeling came over me again. At once I saw burning airplanes and shadows like large crosses all around. The smell of smoke and the crackling of burning wood annoyed me. The darkness clutched at me. I couldn't stand it any longer.

"I've got to get out for a while," I said.

Mother understood. She reminded me of the curfew as she closed the door behind me. I walked across the street to see if Roy Verkerk was home. He was ready to come outside. He always wanted to get out of the house. He was restless and aggressive because the Germans had taken his father after they accused him of listening to the B.B.C.

Roy's father hated Germans. Whenever he approached a soldier in the street he spat on the ground and passed him on the opposite side of the street in a wide circle. He despised the Germans more than cabbage soup. Meneer Verkerk was the roughest and hulkiest man on the street. He walked with big steps and Roy always had to run to keep up with him. When he talked you could hear him almost a block away. I don't think Verkerk could keep a secret from anyone. When he met someone he knew in the street he shook hands and put one big hand on the other's shoulder like a lion clawing at small game. One night he was drunk when I heard him outside howling, "Darling we are growing old. . . ." Peeking through the window of my bedroom, which was on the street side, I saw him standing right in front of me—a giant hugging the lantern post. Then he swore, awful growling curses, and staggered homewards.

Roy liked his father. He said you should know him better and you would find he had a heart for people. He did not know where his father was, but he was determined to find out.

We started out as usual, scout-step. Forty steps running, twenty walking. At the end of the street we slowed down.

"They say four men got killed down East Indies Lane," Roy said. "Let's go and look. Do you suppose my dad. . . ." He hesitated. "Do you suppose he could. . . ?"

"I don't know," I said.

I remembered seeing a dead dog run over by a car. Its guts lay outside on the street. There was blood running out of the open wounds. I had felt like throwing up at once. My stomach had growled and felt as if it was turning upside down. A policeman came by and shot the dog. My head swam. I had never seen a dead human. I had asked mother about it and she said it was the same for people.

I wanted to run back home and quietly sit down and watch mother mend socks in the family room. But I was afraid Roy would think me a coward, so I kept walking toward a dark looming unknown.

We turned into Queen's Lane. There was not a single tree left. People had once come here for a walk because of the splendor of trees and the rare birds that nested in them. They came to feed the pigeons and sit around chatting on wooden benches and listen to the songs of nightingales. But during the cold winter they had come at night and chopped down the trees and stripped the wood off the benches. The birds had left one by one as if they sensed the presence of an eagle overhead. The night was filled with hatred and fear of death.

"Do you ever dream?" Roy said.

"Sometimes I do," I said.

"I dream often. I see a row of dead trees and it's dark all around; the wind rushes through the trees and they fall down. I am fighting the storm but it keeps howling. I see a face in the tree. I pull and pull, but the tree won't move. I scream loud and it wakes me up. Then I'm scared."

"Do you think they will shoot him?"

"I don't know. It frightens me."

Streetcar number thirteen came down the bend on East Indies Lane. We hurried to the safety island and waited until the conductor blew his whistle. As the car began to move, we jumped on the outside stepping board and hung on until the next stop. We jumped off the riding car and ran across the street. The conductor made a fist at us.

The street was divided by two streetcar tracks. Beyond the lanes on each side were rows of houses, broken by a florist stand on the one side and a liquor store on the other side. We walked close to the houses for about five minutes and came to the liquor store.

There were four shrouds on the sidewalk where the men had been shot. We asked a lady what happened but she said we were too young. So we turned to a man of maybe fifty who sat by one of the shrouds shaking his head. He leaned his elbows on his knees and his head rested in his hands while his fingers moved restlessly through his hair. I felt sorry for the man, so I tapped him on the shoulder and asked what happened. His face was pale and his lips were thin when he looked up. He hardly seemed to hear what I said. So I asked again. Then his lips moved slowly. In a low and toneless voice he said,

"These men were picked up from the street at random by the Germans. They said someone dynamited a German car. This one here was my son." He pointed to the body near where he sat. A tear of anger mixed with grief burned in my eye. I quickly wiped it off. There were a lot of flowers thrown on the shrouds. A woman with a black veil stooped over a body, making the sign of the cross.

"Disperse!" shouted a German soldier. We pulled the old man away from the body of his son and hid him behind a privet hedge. The old man was wailing. We saw the soldier carry a sign. He nailed it onto the brick wall just above the bodies. Then he clicked his heels, and said, "Sieg Heil!" but nobody moved. He took his seat behind the driver. When the jeep drove off we came out to look. The sign was in German; curly letters in black print. Underneath was a translation in smaller letters. It said that death would come to anyone who sabotaged the Third Reich as these four men had.

Something inside of me was pounding so hard I could almost hear it. My head felt funny. I closed my eyes because I couldn't see for a moment. When I opened them again I saw long white hair curling over the collar of a shirt. I recognized Roy.

"You were staggering," he said.

"I felt dizzy," I said.

We walked up East Indies Lane, keeping close to the houses as it was past curfew time.

"Father was not there," said Roy, "I looked under the shrouds." He looked pale and tired.

"I'm sorry," I said clumsily. "What did they look like?"

"They looked all blue and purplish red. One had his eyes open and stared right at me. I felt like screaming and running away. But I wanted to be sure so I looked at all of them. Let's get out of here."

We hurried down the street; away from those shrouds and smelling bodies and toward home where there was light and air. The street looked gory and it smelled of decomposing garbage. My nose was itching so I wiped it with my sleeve. There was a shadow sitting in the gutter by the sidewalk. When we came closer we saw it was a man. He was taking off his shoe. We stopped, hoping he would not see us. He held the shoe in both hands and began chewing the leather sole. His face was unshaven, his jawbones stuck out and his eyes were deeply sunken. In that position the man looked like a rat in a garbage can. I held my breath, as I thought I recognized him.

"Is that Meneer Manier?" I said.

"That's him," said Roy.

Mr. Manier was our schoolteacher. If anyone would make one mistake in a French theme, the teacher would have him rewrite the whole theme. He always talked about manners. The boys would have to open the door when girls would come into the class. The way he chewed was embarrassing. Fortunately he did not see us. A gnawing hunger kept his senses spellbound on his shoe sole. I took a deep breath and slowly released the air again. Then we ran past the man.

We came to the Shell station, which was about three blocks away from home. There was no gasoline but it sold charcoal instead. Most cars were equipped with a stovelike contraption that was kept going on charcoal. The gases coming from the heated wood were conducted into a fire chamber which created the combustion necessary for compression in the motor. At least, that's how Mister Brandt, the mechanic, explained it to us. He said that the German car that had been exploded had dynamite in its firechamber. The dynamite ignited when the Germans started the car and blew them into eternity, car and all.

We were almost past the gas station when I heard the sound of spiked boots coming from behind. We took off our shoes to kill their sound on the pavement. We stepped on, faster and faster. The footsteps kept following. We ran behind the gas station and hid behind an abandoned jeep. The steps kept coming. We sweated out every step. They stood still and we saw the silhouette of a soldier. He listened but he couldn't hear a thing and it was too dark to see us. When he was at a safe distance we fled into the swamp next to the gas station.

We slunk through the reeds, stopping every few steps to hear whether the German was still around. Roy coughed, making short, hacky noises.

"Wass ist loss," a voice shouted into the darkness. We kept quiet as we fell down in the reeds. A flashlight beam circled above our heads. We didn't move. Then the light went off again. The soldier mumbled something to himself. He stood there for what seemed an hour and then we heard him slowly walk away. We got up and moved forward on hands and knees.

"Ouch!" cried Roy.

"Shh! What's the matter?"

"My leg. I hit my leg." His hand reached for the thing he had walked into.

"What is it?"

"I don't know. I can't get it to move." He pulled at an object that was stuck in the mud.

"Let me help you." Our hands tightened around the cold thing as our muscles exerted their strength. We pulled and pulled, and at last the thing gave in a little, but we could not hold on to it, so we let go again. We took a deep breath and counted, "One, two, three. . . ," and pulled together with a big jerk.

"Roy! Look!" I said half aloud.

"Shh! What's up?" said Roy.

"It's a boot and there's something in it."

"Let me feel it."

"It feels like frog's eggs."

"Do you suppose . . .

"Suppose what?"

"Do you suppose . . . "

"Maybe. What shall we do now?"

"You hold on while I go and get Mister Brandt."

"Okay. Hurry back."

I held the boot with both hands, until my muscles were getting stiff and sore. There was mud and dead leaves all over the boot and I didn't dare to think of what it might be. Then I heard noises in the swamp and saw the silhouettes of a man and a boy approaching.

Roy showed Mister Brandt the spot. Then we all pulled. Slowly a leg sucked out of the mud, and another; then a body, but it slid back in the mud again as it slipped out of our hands.

"Run to the gas station and get a rope," Mister Brandt said. Roy had a strange look on his face when he crawled out of the swamp and ran into the darkness.

"Let's try again," said Mister Brandt after he had wiped his hands on the back of his pants. I stood close to the left leg and pulled as hard as I could. Mister Brandt pulled on the other leg, much harder, and then the rest of the body and the head came out. When the head came out, water and mud gushed all over us.

"I'll be . . . " said Mister Brandt. I felt the hand that was next to me and it felt like playdough. My back and shoulders rippled as if they were agitated by a cold wind. Then I turned my head and looked at the face. The sight cut my breath. The eyes were staring into nowhere. I turned my face and covered it with my hands. It felt as if it were raining inside of me and filling me up. I wanted to shout for help but there was only a gargle in my throat. I wanted to run away but I didn't have the strength to get up.

Mister Brandt put his hand on my shoulder.

"Never seen a dead man before, boy?"

I shook my head no.

"That's how it is. It's the same for all people."

I cringed at the sound of the words. It echoed in the rustling of the Lombardy poplars and in the widow willows. It was dark all around and I felt part of the darkness. I looked at the trees from where the sound came and saw a faint light behind the trees.

"It's his pa!" I cried and ran into the swamp, and out of the swamp, and down the street and into a big open door.

"Slow down, boy!" A man in a black suit stood in front of me with his arms half outstretched. I stopped and walked around one arm slowly down the grey drab marble floor, without looking up. The floor felt cold under my feet and there were tombstones all around. I heard the sound of a coin dropping in a metal lined box behind me, and then a Gregorian chant from the side. And lonesome, marble stones whispered, "It is the same for all people, all people. . . ."

I turned around and walked back toward the door. I tied my shoes around my belt and, running from house to house for fear of being caught by the German night patrol, I went straight home.

The door opened before I could reach the bell. Dad had come home already and was waiting behind the door. He put his hand on my shoulder. It felt warm and strong. I turned my head a little and looked at the blue veins swollen on the back of the hand and at the little scars on the sides of the half-bent fingers. The scars were black from shoveling coal and there were little white lines where a pen knife had cleaned the dirt from under the fingernails.

"You look pale. Where are your shoes?" dad said. "Where have you been? Your mother and I were worried about you."

I told him about the street and about the swamp and what happened there. Dad put his arm around my shoulders as if he wanted to protect me and be proud of me at the same time. I felt a sensation of blood rushing through my head. Then I looked at his face.

"You know what you must do," he said.

"Yes," I said, "I'll go and tell him before he finds out himself."

What would you tell Roy if you were the speaker in this story?

What options does the boy have after he tells his father about what he's found?

Why does he decide to do the task himself?

Becoming

Utopia

Utopia is a pretty place—
Well regulated.
The thought is excellent—
Perhaps it would work
If everyone were a Plato . . .

But still . . .
  I like a place
    Where I can be myself.

Ralph H. Fox

"Utopia" is an ideal society in which everyone has just the right place. How would that place be different from a place "Where I can be myself"?

A Day No Pigs Would Die

Robert Newton Peck

Papa had been right. The apple crop was lean. The weather had turned colder, and we were lucky to get a few Baldwins and Jonathans barreled for wintering in the cellar. The apples that we did harvest were not large, and many had worm holes. The one tree that had died was our greening tree, one that produced smaller apples that were green and very tart. Pie apples. This winter there would be no pies.

Twice, Papa had seen a buck and several doe upon the ridge. But each time he got the shotgun and slug shells ready, the deer were gone. Jacob Henry's father got a buck. So did Ira Long, who worked for Mrs. Bascom. One of the men who farmed for Ben Tanner got a doe. But Papa didn't have a deer rifle, only a shotgun with ball loads. He had to get close for a shot.

He still-hunted early almost every morning, hoping to get a buck deer before it was time to go to work. No luck. Once he even sat for four hours in a cold rain, waiting. He coughed after that; a deep rattling cough that made him hang on to things. But the worst thing was when his lungs got so bad he stopped sleeping with Mama. He slept in the barn. It was warmer there, with Daisy and Solomon both enclosed in a cozy area.

The first snow came. It wasn't very heavy; and when the next day's sun broke through, it all melted away. But more would follow.

Pinky did not have a litter of pigs. She was bred and she was barren. And she ate too much to keep as a pet. Samson had mounted her twice, and there was no litter. Nothing. And no estrus. She never came to heat, not even once.

It all ended early one morning on a dark December day. It was Saturday and there was no school. After chores, Papa and I came in for breakfast. I tried to down a big bowl of hot steaming oatmeal, but it tasted like soap. And the fresh warm milk from Daisy's pail was flat. I couldn't swallow it. Papa just sat at the kitchen table, fingering a pipe that he couldn't smoke and looking at a breakfast he couldn't eat. He finally got up from the table to look through the window. Outside, the dark of the moon was just softening into first light. When he turned round to me, his face was sober.

"Rob, let's get it done."

I didn't ask what. I just knew. And so did Mama and Aunt Carrie, because as Papa and I were getting our coats on to go outside, they both came over and pretended to help bundle me up.

There had been an inch of light snow the night before. Just enough to cover the ground the way Mama would flour her cake board. I followed Papa out to where we kept the tools, and I stood there watching as he sharpened the knives on the wheel. The sticking knife was short and blunt, with a curved blade. The edge he put to it was extra sharp. He pulled on some heavy rubber boots in the barn, and tied a sheath of leather around his middle, for an apron. We were ready.

Toting some of the tools and a spine saw, I followed him out of the shed and around to the south side of the barn, to where old Solomon and the capstan had pulled the corn cratch, Pinky's house. Inside she was lying all curled up warm in the clean straw. It was a soft warm smell.

"Come on, Pinky," I tried to say in a cheerful way. "It's morning." But my throat seemed to catch and the words just wouldn't come out. I nudged her with my foot, but finally had to take a switch and make her get to her feet. She came to me, muzzle pointed into my leg. Her curly tail was moving about like it was glad the day had started. People say pigs don't feel. And that they don't wag their tails. All I know is that Pinky sure knew who I was and her tail did too.

While Papa lit a fire to boil the water, I pushed her out of the crib and into a box pen, the same one that she'd been in when bred to Samson, the neighbor's pig. She balked at the gate, and I had to hit her hard with the stick a few times to move her forward. It probably hurt her, but what did it matter now.

Following her into the box pen, we closed the gate by

sliding the bars across. I got down on my knees in the snow and put my arms around her big white neck, smelling her good solid smell.

Pinky, I said to myself, try and understand. If there was any other way. If only Papa had got a deer this fall. Or if I was old enough to earn money. If only . . .

"Help me, boy," said Papa. "It's time."

He put his tools on the ground, keeping only a three-foot crowbar. Neither one of us wore gloves, and I knew how cold that crowbar felt. I'd carried it, and it was colder than death.

"Back away," he said.

"Papa," I said, "I don't think I can."

"That's not the issue, Rob. We have to."

Standing up, I moved away from Pinky as Papa went to her head. She just stood there in the fresh snow, looking at my feet. I saw Papa get a grip on the crowbar, and raise it high over his head. It was then I closed my eyes, and my mouth opened like I wanted to scream for her. I waited. I waited to hear the noise that I finally heard.

It was a strong, crushing noise, that you hear only when an iron stunner bashes in a pig's skull. I hated Papa that moment. I hated him for killing her, and hated him for every pig he ever killed in his lifetime . . . for hundreds and hundreds of butchered hogs.

"Hurry," he said.

I opened my eyes and went to her. She was down in the snow. Moving, breathing, but down. I helped roll her over on her back, standing astride her and holding her two forelegs straight up in the air. With his left hand Papa pushed her chin down so that the top of her snout touched the ground. His right hand held the blunt knife with the curved blade. He stuck her throat deep and way back, moving the knife back through the neck toward himself, cutting the main neck artery. Her blood gushed, bubbled out in heaving floods. Some of it went on my boots. I wanted to run, and cry and scream. But I just stood there, helping to hold her kicking.

It was all so quiet, like Christmas morning. As Papa continued to draw the pork, I held the feet firm and up. The blood was still pumping out of her, and the ground beneath our feet was spotted with hot pig blood steaming on the cold snow.

Between my ankles I could feel her body quiver in death. I had to look away. So as Papa worked on her, I held fast, staring at the old corn cratch that had once been Pinky's home.

Papa worked quiet and quick. The guts got drawn out and were there on the cold ground in a hot misty mass. Then we each put a hook in the jaws and dragged the bloody body into boiling water. It was boiled, scraped free of all hair and scurf, and sawed in half.

Papa was breathing the way no man or beast should breathe. I had never seen any man work as fast. I knew his hands must of been just about froze off; but he kept working, with no gloves. At last he stopped, pushing me away from the pork and turning me around so as my back was to it. He stood close by, facing me, and his whole body was steaming wet with work.

I couldn't help it. I started thinking about Pinky. My sweet big clean white Pinky who followed me all over. She was the only thing I ever really owned. The only thing I could point to and say . . . *mine.* But now there was no Pinky. Just a sopping wet lake of red slush. So I cried.

"Oh, Papa. My heart's broke."

"So is mine," said Papa. "But I'm happy you're a man."

I just broke down, and Papa let me cry it all out. I

just sobbed and sobbed with my head up toward the sky and my eyes closed, hoping God would hear it.

"That's what being a man is all about, boy. It's just doing what's got to be done."

I felt his big hand touch my face, and it wasn't the hand that killed hogs. It was almost as wet as Mama's. His hand was rough and cold, and as I opened my eyes to look at it, I could see that his knuckles were dripping with pig blood. It was the hand that just butchered Pinky. He did it. Because he had to. Hated to and had to. And he knew that he'd never have to say to me that he was sorry. His hand against my face, trying to wipe away my tears, said it all. His cruel pig-sticking fist with its thick fingers so lightly on my cheek.

I couldn't help it. I took his hand to my mouth and held it against my lips and kissed it. Pig blood and all. I kissed his hand again and again, with all its stink and fatty slime of dead pork. So he'd understand that I'd forgive him even if he killed me.

I was still holding his hand as he straightened up tall against the gray winter sky. He looked down at me and then he looked away. With his free arm he raked the sleeve of his work shirt across his eyes. It was the first time I'd ever seen him do it.

The only time.

Father and I

Pär Lagerkvist

I remember one Sunday afternoon when I was about ten years old, Daddy took my hand and we went for a walk in the woods to hear the birds sing. We waved good-bye to mother, who was staying at home to prepare supper, and so couldn't go with us. The sun was bright and warm as we set out briskly on our way. We didn't take this bird-singing too seriously, as though it was something special or unusual. We were sensible people, Daddy and I. We were used to the woods and the creatures in them, so we didn't make any fuss about it. It was just because it was Sunday afternoon and Daddy was free. We went along the railway line where other people aren't allowed to go, but Daddy belonged to the railway and had a right to. And in this way we came direct into the woods and did not need to take a round-about way. Then the bird song and all the rest began at once. They chirped in the bushes; hedge-sparrows, thrushes, and warblers; and we heard all the noises of the little creatures as we came into the woods. The ground was thick with anemones, the birches were dressed in their new leaves, and the pines had young, green shoots. There was such a pleasant smell everywhere. The mossy ground was steaming a little, because the sun was shining upon it. Everywhere there was life and noise; bumble-bees flew out of their holes, midges circled where it was damp. The birds shot out of the bushes to catch them and then dived back again. All of a sudden a train came rushing along and we had to go down the embankment. Daddy hailed the driver with two fingers to his Sunday hat: the driver saluted and waved his hand. Everything seemed on the move. As we went on our way along the sleepers which lay and oozed tar in the sunshine, there was a smell of everything, machine oil and almond blossom, tar and heather, all mixed. We took big steps from sleeper to sleeper so as not to step among the stones, which were rough to walk on, and wore your shoes out. The rails shone in the sunshine. On both sides of the line stood the telephone poles that sang as we went by them. Yes! That was a fine day! The sky was absolutely clear. There wasn't a single cloud to be seen: there just couldn't be any on a day like this, according to what Daddy said. After a while we came to a field of oats on the right side of the line, where a farmer, whom we knew, had a clearing. The oats had grown thick and even; Daddy looked at it knowingly, and I could feel that he was satisfied. I didn't understand that sort of thing much, because I was born in town. Then we came to the bridge over the brook that mostly hadn't much water in it, but now there was plenty. We took hands so that we shouldn't fall down between the sleepers. From there it wasn't far to the railway gate-keeper's little place, which was quite buried in green. There were apple trees and gooseberry bushes right close to the house. We went in there, to pay a visit, and they offered us milk. We looked at the pigs, the hens, and the fruit trees, which were in full blossom, and then we went on again. We wanted to go to the river, because there it was prettier than anywhere else. There was something special about the river, because higher up stream it flowed past Daddy's old home. We never liked going back before we got to it, and, as usual, this time we got there after a fair walk. It wasn't far to the next station, but we didn't go on there. Daddy just looked to see whether the signals were right. He thought of everything. We stopped by the river, where it flowed broad and friendly in the sunshine, and the thick leafy trees on the banks mirrored themselves in the calm water. It was all so fresh and bright. A breeze came from the little lakes higher up. We climbed down the bank, went a little way along the very edge. Daddy showed me the fishing spots. When he was a boy he used to sit there on the stones and wait for perch all day long. Often he didn't get a single bite, but it was a delightful way to spend the day. Now he never had time. We played about for some time by the side of the river, and threw in pieces of bark that the current carried away, and we threw stones to see who could throw farthest. We were, by nature, very merry and cheerful, Daddy and I. After a while we felt a bit tired. We thought we had played enough, so we started off home again.

Then it began to get dark. The woods were changed. It wasn't quite dark yet, but almost. We made haste. Maybe mother was getting anxious, and waiting supper. She was always afraid that something might happen, though nothing had. This had been a splendid day. Everything had been just as it should, and we were satisfied with it all. It was getting darker and darker, and the trees were so queer. They stood and listened for the sound of our footsteps, as though they didn't know who we were. There was a glow-worm under one of them. It lay down there in the dark and stared at us. I held Daddy's hand tight, but he didn't seem to notice the strange light: he just went on. It was quite dark when we came to the bridge over the stream. It was roaring down underneath us as if it wanted to swallow us up, as the ground seemed to open under us. We went along the sleepers carefully, holding hands tight so that we shouldn't fall in. I thought Daddy would carry me over, but he didn't say anything about it. I suppose he wanted me to be like him, and not think anything of it. We went on. Daddy was so calm in the darkness, walking

with even steps without speaking. He was thinking his own thoughts. I couldn't understand how he could be so calm when everything was so ghostly. I looked round scared. It was nothing but darkness everywhere. I hardly dared to breathe deeply, because then the darkness comes into one, and that was dangerous, I thought. One must die soon. I remember quite well thinking so then. The railway embankment was very steep. It finished in black night. The telephone posts stood up ghostlike against the sky, mumbling deep inside as though someone were speaking, way down in the earth. The white china hats sat there scared, cowering with fear, listening. It was all so creepy. Nothing was real, nothing was natural, all seemed a mystery. I went closer to Daddy, and whispered: "Why is it so creepy when it's dark?"

"No child, it isn't creepy," he said, and took my hand.

"Oh, yes, but it is, Daddy."

"No, you mustn't think that. We know there is a God, don't we?" I felt so lonely, so abandoned. It was queer that it was only me that was frightened, and not Daddy. It was queer that we didn't feel the same about it. And it was queerer still that what he said didn't help, didn't stop me being frightened. Not even what he said about God helped. The thought of God made one feel creepy too. It was creepy to think that He was everywhere here in the darkness, down there under the trees, and in the telephone posts that mumbled so—probably that was Him everywhere. But all the same one could never see Him.

We went along silently, each of us thinking his own thoughts. My heart felt cramped as though the darkness had come in and was squeezing it.

Then, when we were in a bend, we suddenly heard a great noise behind us. We were startled out of our thoughts. Daddy pulled me down the embankment and held me tight, and a train rushed by; a black train. The lights were out in all the carriages, as it whizzed past us. What could it be? There shouldn't be any train now. We looked at it, frightened. The furnace roared in the big engine, where they shovelled in coal, and the sparks flew out into the night. It was terrible. The driver stood so pale and immovable, with such a stony look in the glare. Daddy didn't recognize him—didn't know who he was. He was just looking ahead as though he was driving straight into darkness, far into darkness, which had no end.

Startled and panting with fear I looked after the wild thing. It was swallowed up in the night. Daddy helped me up on to the line, and we hurried home. He said, "That was strange! What train was that I wonder? And I didn't know the driver either." Then he didn't say any more.

I was shaking all over. That had been for me—for my sake. I guessed what it meant. It was all the fear which would come to me, all the unknown: all that Daddy didn't know about, and couldn't save me from. That was how the world would be for me, and the strange life I should live; not like Daddy's, where everyone was known and sure. It wasn't a real world, or a real life;—it just rushed burning into the darkness which had no end.

I've Gotta Be Free

Whether I'm right or whether I'm wrong
Whether I find a place in this world or never belong,
I've gotta be me! I've gotta be me!
What else can I be but what I am?
I want to live! not merely survive!
And I won't give up this dream of life that keeps me
alive.
I've gotta be me! I've gotta be me!

I'll go it alone. That's how it must be.
I can't be right for somebody else if I'm not right for
me.
I've gotta be free! I've gotta be free!
Daring to try to do it or die! I've gotta be me!

Walter Marks

What's your reaction to this song?

Compare this with "The Father." Which attitude gets closest to yours?

The Distant Drum

I am not a metaphor or symbol.
This you hear is not the wind in the trees,
Nor a cat being maimed in the street.
I am being maimed in the street.
It is I who weep, laugh, feel pain or joy,
Speak this because I exist.
This is my voice.
These words are my words,
My mouth speaks them,
My hand writes—
I am a poet.
It is my fist you hear
Beating against your ear.

Calvin C. Hernton

Why is this poem a "distant drum"?

What is the "fist" you'd like to "beat against" people's "ears"?

Three-Minute Friendships

Dana Tregilgas

Of all the days in the week, Mondays are the worst. They are the slowest and most unfriendly. I always feel as if we've been out of school for a long vacation, and Monday is the day to come back.

I'm in no hurry to get down to English class. I hate to leave this room. It's the warmest room in the school. Too bad some of its heat won't follow me downstairs. The last of the girls are finally setting off—down to Room 10.

"You know, I didn't do any homework this weekend," boasts Carol, "I didn't have time." Several other girls make the same statement.

That's what I was afraid of, but it's not a surprise. Carol rarely does her homework. She usually manages to get by some other way. That's the main reason why I'm in no hurry to get down to English. If I wait long enough, Sister Martha might be there. Then Carol won't be hanging around next to my desk to take a look at my homework. . . .

September was two long months ago. I was kneeling on the floor putting books beneath my desk before the start of history class. Judy paused at my side. I expected some sort of greeting. Instead she began with, "Say, is that your homework paper? Let me see it for a minute?"

I mumbled an agreement. Then looking up, I saw that Judy was gone and so was my paper. I motioned to her that I wanted my paper back, but the bell rang. Chaos began. After ten minutes of watching my paper being passed from one girl to another, I got it back.

Judy was eager to answer homework questions. I

looked at my own paper and followed along. Her answers not only started like mine, but also ended like mine, and had the same words in the middle! A strange feeling hit my stomach. I was disgusted with myself.

Toward the middle of September, it happened again. This time it was Karen who caught me between classes. She ran her long, perfect fingernail down the edge of my notebook. Karen wanted a favor, and I knew it. "Let me see your grammar homework for a minute?" I hesitated. "Come on," she said, "don't be such a Holy Joe." That hurt, and I gave in.

The grammar papers came back the next day—mine with a 90 per cent. Karen had the same, so did her three best friends. Sister Martha talked about the seventh sentence. Everybody seemed to have made the same mistake. Karen winked, and one of her friends smirked at me. I knew what my biggest mistake was. It made me mad. . . .

There are many days, especially Mondays like today, when I want to leave my finished assignments at home. I want to burn them, or drop my notebook behind a radiator—anything to avoid those sweet voices that "just want to take a quick look" at my homework. I'm sick of these three-minute friendships between bells.

Just about everybody is down on the second floor now. I don't want to arrive with any time to spare before class begins. Besides, it's much warmer here on the landing near the silver radiator. The loud voices from Room 10 make me feel sick. The bell should ring in a second. I'll have to go down.

Every step is difficult. I could tell Sister that I don't feel well. She might send me home. It's true. I don't feel well, but going home won't be a cure. I'll just try to slip into the room without being noticed. But Carol sees me.

"Oh, there you are." The words sting my ears. "Let me see your paper for a second, huh?"

I'll sit in that desk next to the radiator. I'm so cold. A tug on my sleeve reminds me that Carol is waiting. Her eyes are impatient.

"No," I answer, and a chill runs through me.

Her eyes jump up to meet mine. Her hand trembles on my arm. "What did you say?"

"I won't let you see my paper. Do your own work."

There. It's done. I don't feel sick any more, but I'm still cold. I need the warm radiator.

In the same situation as the narrator of the story, what would you have done?

How obligated are you to help others? Should you ever do their work for them?

Haiku

The morning after
storm, the land yields sea treasure.

Trouble my water.

Phyllis Zylstra McGuinness

Hard Row

Glenn Meeter

"Just put him right to work," my father said. The Sneller family looked at me—twelve years old, long-waisted, pimples, wearing a baseball cap and T shirt and tennis shoes, my buttocks braced against my father's station wagon. They stood, all four of them, next to the corn rows, each one leaning on a hoe. The boy and girl were maybe nine and ten years old, shorter than I, but stocky. They wore sloppily fitting flannel shirts, dirty work shoes and straw hats. Mrs. Sneller looked like her children but wore a red bandanna around her head; she blew her nose in another just like it. None of them answered my father.

Old man Sneller was part Indian, my father had told me by way of juicing me up for the job; but his eyes were pale and red-rimmed and his stubble of beard (which on my father showed only at night, never in the morning) was white. He stood straight, however, like an Indian. His denim jacket looked as if it had never been washed, the original blue darkened with caked dirt and grease; he wore a black derby with a red feather in the band. He was staring at my T shirt, where a cute bear cub was swinging a bat—or perhaps it was at my unprotected, undeveloped chest. From the start, I felt he despised me.

"Good-by, Son." My father reached over and gave me a clumsy pat on the back.

"Good-by." I walked slowly toward the Snellers, slapping my left palm with my right fist as though I were wearing a baseball glove. The ground was hard brown lumps like rocks; I stumbled to my knees. Mrs. Sneller bent forward and I was afraid she would help me up; instead, she looked at her husband. He didn't move.

"That's all right," my father said, going quickly to the driver's side and getting into the car. "He'll be all right. Just don't be afraid to make him work; that's what he's here for!"

Sneller jerked his hoe suddenly into the dirt. "Don't worry about that," he said, and the other Snellers laughed suddenly and sharply. They all began walking toward the corn rows, swinging their hoes like walking sticks. I followed, careful where I put my feet. The station wagon rolled over the hill in puffs of gray dust, and then I heard it whine away into silence out on the county trunk, invisible behind rows and rows of corn.

It was my first job, arranged by my father because I had been moping (my mother's word for it) around the house. We were new in Wisconsin, and the town library where we lived, open six hours a week, had no books I hadn't read. There was no swimming pool, no baseball—no park, even—no tennis court or golf course; and any boys who might have been my friends were themselves working, usually on a relative's farm. I listened to baseball broadcasts and the rest of the time I moped, getting on my mother's nerves. She in turn got on my father's. When I broke a neighbor's garage window, playing catch with myself, she told my father, who called up my great-uncle, who owned the farm that the Snellers rented—it was a long-distance call, back to Chicago—and I had my first job.

Do him a world of good, my father said. On those hot July nights when we all lay sleepless upstairs with open doors and windows, I could hear him reassuring my mother. Often after prodding my father into action, she had to be reassured about the results. I had never done any hard work, she pointed out. She wanted me to go to college, become a doctor, maybe a lawyer. She didn't want me mingling with a lot of roughnecks; what she had in mind was more like, say, a summer camp. My father, a salesman, was more persuasive. Fresh air. Exercise. Sunshine. Get his feet on the ground. Meat on his bones. Hair on his chest. School of hard knocks, experience the best teacher. See how the other half lives. Among the books I had read before exhausting the library was *T-Model Tommy,* the story of a boy who built his own trucking business, starting only with a T-Model Ford and his bare hands. My father's phrases reminded me of that book. Having sympathized as strongly as I did with Tommy, the hero, over his rival, Bruce, who had money, cars, college and all the advantages, I was confident of success on the job. Perhaps I was no Tommy, but I certainly was no Bruce. Borne up by my father's phrases floating to me down the open hallway, I floated off to sleep.

Sneller gave me a hoe and some gloves, that first morning, off the back of his pickup truck. "Thank you," I said when he handed me the hoe, and he laughed—a short, sharp laugh, like a curse. I didn't thank him for the gloves. We each took a row, five in all: the mother, the girl, Sneller, me, the boy. Sneller was in the middle so that he could pull along the weak links—me and the girl.

"Keep up," he said. "Hard row, we keep you up. Easy row, you keep us up." So I started; he had been working while he spoke and was already several yards ahead.

I tried to hoe like Sneller. Mrs. Sneller used a short, near-vertical chop, drawing the weeds toward her feet; the boy and the girl used a variety of strokes, swinging, sawing, chopping—effective enough, though clumsy; but

Sneller's hoe scarcely seemed to move. He appeared to be going for a stroll, the hoe busy at his side of its own volition, like an obedient dog at heel, trained to attack weeds. It made a hard, singing sound, *ssst, ching!* and the vines and stalks trailed behind him, roots up in the furrow where they belonged, a green wake following his tough, dirty boots. I did not have a hard row, as near as I could tell, but after half an hour he had done most of it. The boy kept me up too, snaking his hoe quickly across, then pausing to look casually back at me and spit on the ground; even the girl kept me up, darting a look of triumph as she sneaked two rows over to cut my weeds. They had flat, dark eyes like their mother; all of them looked more Indian than Sneller did. But he moved like an Indian.

I stumbled when I walked. My tennis shoes were full of dirt, though the ground beneath felt too hard to crumble. My ankles ached. My side ached from tugging and twisting. My hoe was clumsy—thinner than a bat or tennis racket, longer than a golf club; I couldn't grip it. The gloves Sneller had given me were hard and shiny with dirt, the fingers all curved; it was like wearing a pair of claws. I stuffed them in my pocket. That was better, but soon I had blisters. The weeds stood up close to the corn and the hoe had to be slid in sideways, like opening a letter on the floor with a long stick; or on the far side, so that I had to cross into Sneller's row to get at them—the corn leaves scratching my face and splashing dew down my T shirt as I moved; or between two stalks in a space just smaller than my hoe head. I would hack away with the short edge and finally, missing, bend down and pull the thing out by hand. My blisters turned green. The worst weed was "creeping Jenny," a vine that crept for yards at a time along the rows; if you struck it anywhere except at the well-hidden root, you came up with a hoeful of air—or, like me, left the hoe behind, snarled in leaves and creepers. "That Jenny is awful stuff," Mrs. Sneller said once, watching me work at it like a blind man probing a pool. Sneller, far ahead, looked back at us, and she moved on. Sometimes after working for minutes at a vine I would finally locate the root, already cut off but still in place; that was where the boy or girl had "helped" me. Sneller always hooked them into his furrow. More and more he let me struggle by myself, falling farther and farther behind; then there would be a period of grace, marked by a double width of weeds in his furrow, where I stumbled ahead gratefully—though I learned to hate these clean spaces as marks of my weakness. I shivered, soaked with dew and sweat; the morning sun burned my face beneath the visor of my cap; gnats pestered my eyes. At the end of the row I sank down against a fence post, careful of barbed wire, conscious only of corn in front of me, cows and cow dung behind, the hot sun above, and beneath me clods of dirt.

"Never done this before, I bet," Mrs. Sneller said. She gave a nervous laugh, looking from me to her husband.

"This is my first job," I said.

The children stared. I wanted to stand up with them, but felt dizzy.

"That's a V-Eight wagon, ain't it," the boy said. Like the others, he looked at his father before speaking. "You lucky! You ever get to drive it?"

I shook my head.

Sneller spat on the ground. "Uncle wants clean corn," he said, moving into the rows. "Uncle don't want no sitting down."

The others moved with him, and I, the only one sitting down, got up and followed.

The rest of the day was corn, a green sea in which I bobbed, keeping my head up; and heat, rising off the leaves in dark, hairy waves, burning my face and neck and frying the curled ridges of my ears; and time measured in endless rows of weeds and corn, or sometimes by the passing blessing of a cloud or a breeze, or by the throbbing of my bones and skin. And most of all it was Sneller. Sneller kept me chained to him, moving me up with a few contemptuous strokes, then dropping me back, a stray behind the herd. Sometimes he paused, his pale eyes on me as I hacked and slashed until I was even, and then turned and left me behind again. I scarcely knew my uncle; I had seldom seen him, and as far as I knew, my family had no reason to think highly of him. I would have disowned him if it would have done any good. But it wouldn't. I could earn Sneller's respect only with the hoe. Easy row, you keep us up. I had mainly easy rows, and still they kept me up. I owed them, I felt; I owed them plenty. Not just for my uncle but for myself. Once I heard them talking, far ahead, and Sneller's laugh; I wondered if they were talking about me. I heard Sneller laugh two other times: when I had said, "Thank you," in the morning, and again at noon, pausing for lunch, when I sat on a Canadian thistle.

"Heck, I told you Uncle don't want no sitting down," he said.

In the afternoon my bowels gave me trouble, and my bladder. Once I saw the boy take a leak in his row, but I didn't dare. I wasted enough time sneezing—gobs of blackened mucus in the white ironed handkerchief. I had to stop, wait for the sneeze, take off the gloves (wearing them again to cover the blisters), get out the hanky, wipe with it, pocket it, replace the gloves, pick up the hoe. All the while I felt Sneller watching. Finally

I asked permission—and got it, from Mrs. Sneller—to use the privy. A dark, narrow phone booth full of flies and stink. I came back determined to lie if they asked me if it was my first time in a privy. Once we paused for a drink, swigging in turn from a Mason jar swathed in burlap. My turn came after Sneller, and he told me to wipe it off. Instead I drank without wiping, manfully lipping the ridged glass. It was the right thing to do; none of the others had wiped, and besides I had nothing to wipe with. He jerked the jar away. "I said wipe it off!" Mrs. Sneller said nothing, looking at the ground. I wiped with my dirty shirt and then drank a small, tepid mouthful.

Later Mrs. Sneller and the girl left to start supper, and then the boy left to start the milking. I worked alone with Sneller, falling behind, hacking desperately to keep up, falling behind. Once, failing to cut a big potato weed, I jerked it out by hand—too hard. I went crashing backward into the opposite row. Sneller, looking back, used a phrase I had never heard before. "You break any more stalks, I'll put your ass in a sling."

My head jerked uncontrollably whenever a car passed on the county trunk. At last the station wagon appeared, and then my father, standing at the end of the row in his white shirt. I kept my eyes on my row, finishing by myself as Sneller waited silently with my father.

"Well, well, here he is! I guess he'll sleep well tonight! Did he work out all right? Don't be too easy on him!" It was the kind of jovial stuff he would say to a teacher of mine, or a coach, so that they could respond, No, no he's all right, he's a good kid.

But not Sneller. "We won't be," he said, flinging our tools into the pickup.

On the way home I stared at the dashboard while my

father asked enthusiastic questions. I said nothing, even when he told me how the Cubs had made out.

"Don't pay too much attention to Sneller," he said after a while. "Uncle Emory says he's kind of an odd guy."

In two weeks my blisters turned into calluses. I learned to wear a flannel shirt, with a collar that turned up and sleeves that rolled down when it got too hot or cold or wet, and two front pockets where I could carry gum, Life-Savers and a Chapstick or a pair of plastic sunglasses. If it got too hot, I took it off and tied it by the sleeves around my waist. I smeared my skin with sunburn oil and insect repellent and I walked with the clodhopper's kneeflexing jounce. I could handle the hoe with or without gloves. I was perhaps as good as the boy or girl—better, I thought. I was working at becoming as good as Sneller.

Gradually I was paying them back. Though I was casual about it—gaining a little ground and then coolly reaching out to leave my hoemarks in someone else's row—such events were what I lived for. It was all I had, once I had mastered the fundamentals of walking, breathing and enduring the hours—that and the small physical pleasures like the shade of a cloud, a drink of water or eating a sandwich. The money Sneller gave me at the end of the week ("You'll take it, won't you?" and when I hesitated, not knowing the right answer, "You're darn right you'll take it!")—the money, twelve dollar bills representing thirty cents times forty hours—meant nothing to me. According to my father it would help pay for my college education; it was going into a "fund" and I should be proud of it. I think he wanted me to paste one of the bills on my wall next to Marty Marion and Phil Cavaretta, like the first dollar earned in a restaurant or dry-cleaning shop. But to me the twelve dollars had nothing to do with what I had done and learned in Sneller's cornfield; it was in the field that I was working out my payments and debts.

Often Sneller stayed away for a morning or afternoon, making hay. We could hear the tractor roaring, sputtering and roaring again over the hill. Those were the best times. We worked slowly, and while the others paused to stare out over the corn to the sunny hills of other farms, I would work ahead, gaining ground, and then lean over and keep them up. Mrs. Sneller was just like the children; all of them seemed to regard these Sneller-free periods as small vacations. They would sneak back to the house on some excuse—water or the privy or the mail—or they would tell jokes.

What's the difference between a cow's tail and a pump handle?

I don't know, I would say. I never knew.

Heck, I'd hate to send *you* for water!

Mrs. Sneller liked to check on what I had in my lunch bag—a disappointment to her, since I insisted, over my mother's protests, that it carry no more than the Snellers' lunch bags did, which meant mainly sliced boloney on store bread (no mayonnaise; it went bad in the heat) and some cookies. (At home, after work, I ate a lot of fruit.) She let the children ask me what my father made per month, how much the car cost and did my mother ever work. I always said I didn't know. She liked to ask about my plans for college and career. I would shrug, trying to imply that I could take college or leave it—which was the truth, but I would have done the same if it hadn't been. I was on my guard, figuring they would tell Sneller whatever I told them. I had enough to work out on my own without being drawn further into the camp of my uncle.

When Sneller appeared, or when the sound of the tractor stopped, everyone shut up and worked. He would appear suddenly, his black derby skimming like a water beetle above the tassels, his face always stubbed and gray and white, his eyes pale and red-rimmed. My father told me he shaved at night and then went out drinking. We would hear his hoe chinking at weeds we had missed, or he would take a new row and overhaul us swiftly and silently, the silence telling us what he thought of our work. I was always sweating when he was in the field no matter how cool the day; and I was always falling behind. My muscles stiffened and I hacked and slashed wildly, losing the competence I gained when he was gone. The others worked faster. I never kept anyone up when Sneller was with us; easy row or hard row, they kept me up instead.

One afternoon it rained, big, bluebellied clouds spattering the leaves and our hats and the earth with fat, slanting drops. Mrs. Sneller said we had to go in. The children left immediately, taking their chance, but I decided to work on. She wasn't my boss; Sneller was. I pretended not to hear. After a moment she left, and I worked on, exhilarated by the cold, swift air and the tossing corn. I had never worked so fast and so well. While they huddled miserably on their sloping porch with its wringer-washer and baby's playpen—there was another child, younger than the others, who got to stay home and watch the baby—and its piles of dirty clothes and sour diapers and spark plugs and dismantled engine blocks, I would finish my row. I would finish all four rows! And when the storm was over I would be back, wet, steaming and cool, and lead them back to work four rows ahead of where they thought they'd be.

Suddenly I heard footsteps, running feet. It was Sneller. I whirled, my hoe in the air, and he seized it as if he thought I would strike him.

"You want to get yourself killed?" It took me a moment to realize he was trying to protect me, not threatening me. He shoved me ahead and we both ran back, through the thunder and wet corn, to the house.

I could have been struck by lightning, the others told me. The highest point in a field could be struck—even a child knew that. They all were disgusted at my stupidity. I was conscious only of owing one more thing—my life—to Sneller.

One day about a week later I got an easy row. Sneller was away in town, but the others weren't talking much. They hadn't talked much to me since my effort in the rain. Still, I was moving ahead. I worked some in the girl's row, then some in the boy's; then, gaining more ground, I even helped Mrs. Sneller. They appeared not to notice. With the least bit of effort I found myself ahead again. I suspected a trick, but they were all working hard. I worked ahead, moving with Sneller-like strides, an Indian in a canoe, propelled irresistibly by my effortless paddle; or a batter on a hot streak, eye on the ball all the way and then *crack* . . .

When I looked back they were twenty, thirty yards behind. *Keep up!* I wanted to shout. I paused, working a bit in their rows—not too much, for I knew that hard rows became easy ones, and vice versa. For the first time since starting my job I felt a sense of power. I didn't want this pleasant option, to help or not to help, to pass away. Whistling, I worked on: *ssst, ching!* The weeds fell before my hoe. Amazingly, my row became easier—a few runners of creeping Jenny, here and there a dandelion or thistle—and even the corn grew conveniently spaced for my hoe; while in their rows, surrounding mine, the vines were stacked thick and green, as if the corn had melted and flowed out over the ground. Perhaps it was the way the cultivator had been set; maybe it had something to do with the planting or the drainage—but as far as I could tell it was an act of God. A supremely easy row, perhaps the world's all-time-record easy row, was laid out for me here on the same principle by which polio or oil gushers, hail or tornadoes or lightning, might strike one farm and not another. It was an easy row, and it was mine. I could do with it what I wanted. When I looked back they were far, far behind, the length of a football field. I had outdistanced them all for a touchdown.

I had another hundred yards to the top of the hill; after that it was downhill to the end. I could turn back now and bring them all up with me. They would be sullen, not wanting to admit I had helped them. Or I could go on by myself. I could finish, working as fast as I could—and then, while they pictured me resting, taking my ease, I would suddenly reappear at the top of the hill, working back down to them like a whirlwind, taking all three rows at once. And there it would be, the work all finished, a gift from me to them—whether they wanted to admit it or not.

I doubled my efforts, digging deep, leaving a trail of damp earth on top of the dry furrow. I would leave a clean row, no cheating to get ahead. Almost immediately my row became harder, both corn and weeds growing thick. I stopped whistling. I worked full speed ahead. The daring of what I was trying to do came over me; I felt them catching up and forced myself not to look back. At the top of the hill I saw another hundred yards to the end—farther than I had thought. Panting, I looked back. Even if somehow, impossibly, they caught me, I thought, we would only be back even; there would be nothing lost.

But there were four heads now in the yellow tassels. The fourth was Sneller's. He was moving fast from row to row, hoeing and hoeing—he was helping the other three. He wasn't even taking his own row! And already he had cut down half the distance.

It was too late to go back. Sneller knew what I had done; he was hoeing like fury. I worked on dumbly, dry-mouthed. *Ass in a sling*, my hoe whispered as I worked; *ass in a sling, ass in a sling.* My knees trembled. I had moments of courage when I still hoped to come back to meet them, Sneller and all, or at least end even; but deep down I knew I was finished. Soon I could hear them, a crashing, crunching, treading sound like a prairie fire or swarm of devouring ants behind me. When they finally came into sight and passed me—bent over, all of them hoeing furiously, the dust rising—I could hardly move my hoe. I couldn't muster saliva to shout, "I was going to come back for you!" They wouldn't have believed me anyway.

"Sit down," I heard Sneller say when they finished, several rods ahead. Sneller tolerated sitting; he never commanded it. I peeked. They were all sitting, not drinking or talking, just sitting, waiting for me. When I finished, head down, ready to sink into the fence row, he started them back again. I followed, winded as I was. I didn't see his face and I didn't look. I had only one consolation—that they had not seen me cry.

But on the way back they did. I had a hard row, or one that seemed hard. I kept falling behind. I was too weak to try to catch up, and Sneller helped the others when they lagged too close to me. He kept them up, not me. But once in a while when I fell back too far, I found the marks of his hoe for five or six yards and a double pile of vines in his furrow. Whenever this happened I would cry. I couldn't put those weeds back and hoe them down myself; it was already done. I had to accept it. I had no choice. I would stumble ahead, crying, though I cried silently. Before the row ended the others had seen my tears; they knew that I was crying, and I knew that they knew.

At the end of the week Sneller gave me my last twelve dollars. My father was there with the station wagon, waiting for me. He was still trying to coax Sneller into small talk. "Well, so that's that, eh? I hope he left the corn clean enough for you!" And then, since Sneller's pause looked as if it was going to be a long one, he said, "I guess he learned a few things this summer!"

"I guess," Sneller said.

Later my father asked me whether I felt like doing this again next summer, now that I'd had the experience. I said no, I didn't think so. Maybe I would get a paper route. Anyway, I had a lot of reading I wanted to do next summer to get ready for high school. I wanted to do well in high school because I planned to go to college. Because I knew, deep in my heart, that I was going to grow up as far away from the Snellers as I could. I was going to find an easy row for myself and never ever come back to help them or keep them up, never, no matter how hard their row was or how hard they cried.

Self-Dependence

Weary of myself, and sick of asking
What I am, and what I ought to be,
At the vessel's prow I stand, which bears me
Forwards, forwards, o'er the starlit sea.

And a look of passionate desire
O'er the sea and to the stars I send:
'Ye who from my childhood up have calm'd me,
Calm me, ah, compose me to the end!

‘Ah, once more,’ I cried, ‘ye stars, ye waters,
On my heart your mighty charm renew;
Still, still let me, as I gaze upon you,
Feel my soul becoming vast like you.’

From the intense, clear, star-sown vault of heaven,
Over the lit sea’s unquiet way,
In the rustling night-air came the answer:
‘Wouldst thou *be* as these are? *Live* as they.

‘Unaffrighted by the silence round them,
Undistracted by the sights they see,
These demand not that the things without them
Yield them love, amusement, sympathy.

‘And with joy the stars perform their shining,
And the sea its long moon-silvered roll;
For self-poised they live, nor pine with noting
All the fever of some differing soul.

‘Bounded by themselves, and unregardful
In what state God’s other works may be,
In their own tasks all their powers pouring,
These attain the mighty life you see.’

O air-born voice! long since, severely clear,
A cry like thine in mine own heart I hear.
‘Resolve to be thyself: and know that he
Who finds himself, loses his misery!’

Matthew Arnold

Contrast the first two lines and the last two lines of this poem. What caused the poet to change?

If

If you can keep your head when all about you
   Are losing theirs and blaming it on you,
If you can trust yourself when all men doubt you,
   But make allowance for their doubting too;
If you can wait and not be tired by waiting,
   Or being lied about, don't deal in lies,
Or being hated, don't give way to hating,
   And yet don't look too good, nor talk too wise:

If you can dream—and not make dreams your master;
   If you can think—and not make thoughts your aim;
If you can meet with Triumph and Disaster
   And treat those two imposters just the same;
If you can bear to hear the truth you've spoken
   Twisted by knaves to make a trap for fools,
Or watch the things you gave your life to, broken,
   And stoop and build 'em up with worn-out tools:

If you can make one heap of all your winnings
   And risk it on one turn of pitch-and-toss,
And lose, and start again at your beginnings
   And never breathe a word about your loss;
If you can force your heart and nerve and sinew
   To serve your turn long after they are gone
And so hold on when there is nothing in you
   Except the will which says to them: "Hold on!"

If you can talk with crowds and keep your virtue,
   Or walk with Kings—nor lose the common touch,
If neither foes nor loving friends can hurt you,
   If all men count with you, but none too much;
If you can fill the unforgiving minute
   With sixty seconds' worth of distance run,

Yours is the earth and everything that's in it,
And—which is more—you'll be a Man, my son!

Rudyard Kipling

What would you add or subtract from Kipling's ideal man?

The Road Not Taken

Two roads diverged in a yellow wood,
And sorry I could not travel both
And be one traveler, long I stood
And looked down one as far as I could
To where it bent in the undergrowth;

Then took the other, as just as fair,
And having perhaps the better claim,
Because it was grassy and wanted wear;
Though as for that the passing there
Had worn them really about the same,

And both that morning equally lay
In leaves no step had trodden black.
Oh, I kept the first for another day!
Yet knowing how way leads on to way,
I doubted if I should ever come back.

I shall be telling this with a sigh
Somewhere ages and ages hence:
Two roads diverged in a wood, and I—
I took the one less traveled by,
And that has made all the difference.

Robert Frost

Did you ever come to a "fork" in your life? Are you happy with the road you took? Why do you think that taking the road "less traveled by" has made "all the difference"?

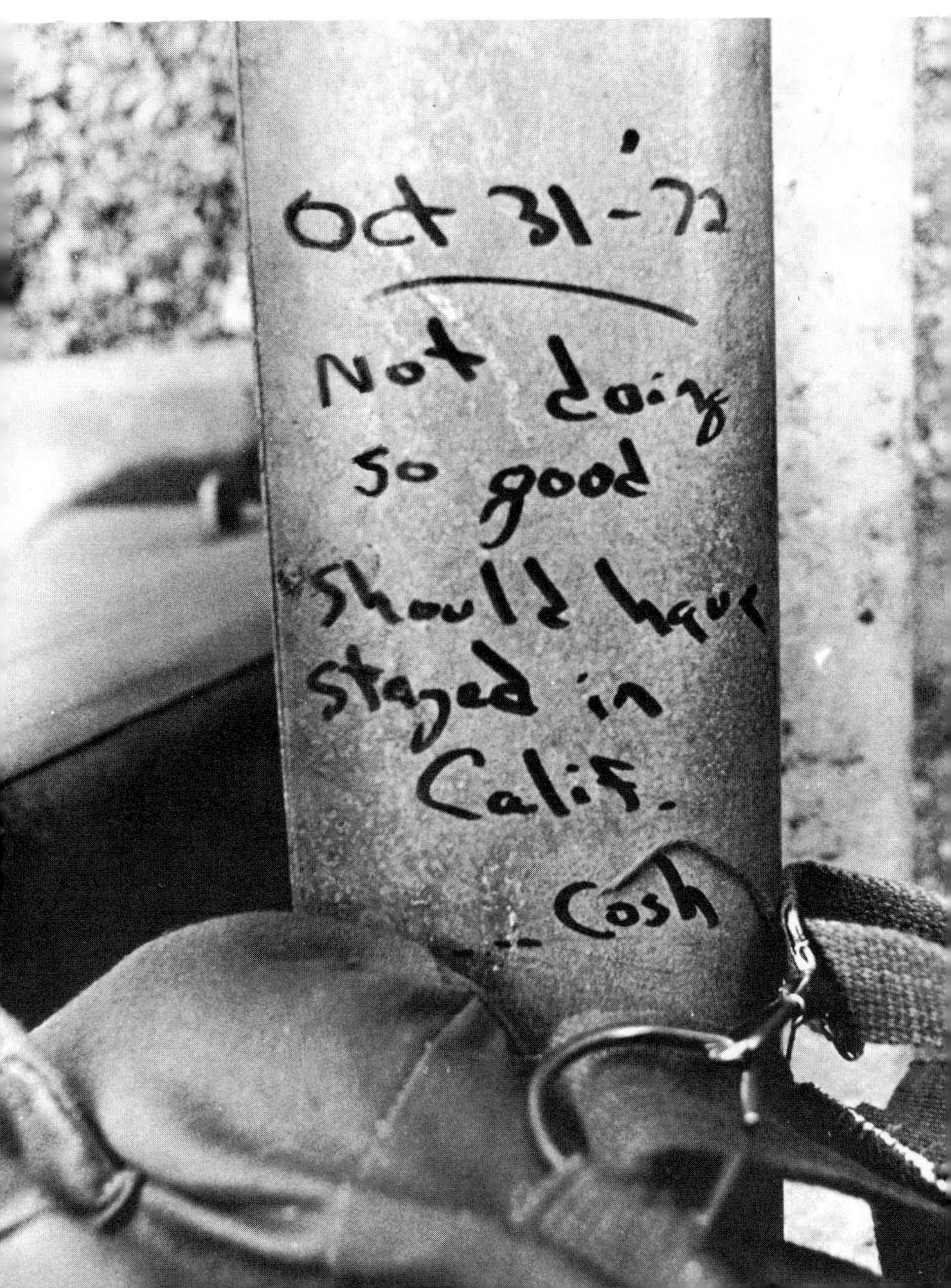

There Will Come a Time

(Ecclesiastes 12)

1 Remember your Creator in the days of your youth,
before the time of trouble comes and the years draw
near when you will say, 'I see no purpose in them.'
2 Remember him before the sun and the light of day give
place to darkness, before the moon and the stars grow
3 dim, and the clouds return with the rain—when the
guardians of the house tremble, and the strong men
stoop, when the women grinding the meal cease work
because they are few, and those who look through the
4 windows look no longer, when the street-doors are shut,
when the noise of the mill is low, when the chirping of
the sparrow grows faint and the song-birds fall silent;
5 when men are afraid of a steep place and the street is
full of terrors, when the blossom whitens on the
almond-tree and the locust's paunch is swollen and
caperbuds have no more zest. For man goes to his
everlasting home, and the mourners go about the streets.
6 Remember him before the silver cord is snapped and the
golden bowl is broken, before the pitcher is shattered at
7 the spring and the wheel broken at the well, before the
dust returns to the earth as it began and the spirit
8 returns to God who gave it. Emptiness, emptiness, says
the Speaker, all is empty.

9 So the Speaker, in his wisdom, continued to teach the
people what he knew. He turned over many maxims in
10 his mind and sought how best to set them out. He chose
his words to give pleasure, but what he wrote was the
11 honest truth. The sayings of the wise are sharp as goads,
like nails driven home; they lead the assembled people,
12 for they come from one shepherd. One further warning,

my son: the use of books is endless, and much study is wearisome.
This is the end of the matter: you have heard it all. 13
Fear God and obey his commands; there is no more to
man than this. For God brings everything we do to 14
judgement, and every secret, whether good or bad.

The New English Bible

Is the message here the same as in Shakespeare's Sonnet 73?